Restructuring and Resizing

Strategies for Social Work and Other Human Services Administrators in Health Care

Candyce S. Berger, Ph.D.

Society for Social Work Administrators in Health Care
American Hospital Association
840 North Lake Shore Drive
Chicago, Illinois 60611

Library of Congress Cataloging-in-Publication Data

Berger, Candyce S.
Restructuring and resizing : strategies for social work and other human services administrators in health care / Candyce Berger.
p. cm.
"AHA catalog no. 187150"—T.p. verso.
Includes bibliographical references.
ISBN 0-87258-626-X
1. Medical social work—United States—Administration.
2. Human services—United States—Administration.
3. Organizational change—United States.
I. Title.
HV687.5.U5B47 1992 92-33264
362.1'0425—dc20 CIP

840 North Lake Shore Drive
Chicago, Illinois 60611

Printed in the U.S.A.
IN1247/2-93/2M

Editorial Services: Carole Bolster
Production: Susan Smith

Contents

Acknowledgments

No piece of work is ever accomplished alone. There are many individuals who contributed to the completion of this book. First, I want to thank the Society for Social Work Administrators in Health Care for giving me this opportunity. I also want to thank Leora Bowden, Harry Bryan, Susan Haikalis, Patricia Meadows, and Kermit Nash for wading through various drafts of the book and providing honest critiques and useful recommendations. My secretary, Evie Dettling, gets a very special thanks for helping me with every phase of the process and protecting my time so that I could complete the book! I also want to thank Robin Johnson, a friend and colleague who worked side-by-side with me through my first resizing experience and provided the intellectual stimulation that planted the first seed to write this book. I also want to recognize the friendship and support of Ellen Stern Kerr and Kimberly McNally, who helped keep me sane and grounded throughout this process.

Finally, I want to thank two of the most important people in my life: my husband, Bill Dethlefs, and my daughter, Hillary Dethlefs. Within the arms of their love and support, I have the courage and strength to seek my dreams. This book is dedicated to Bill and Hillary, for without them life just wouldn't be as much fun.

Chapter 1

Setting the Context for Change

Restructuring and Resizing Defined

The need for radical change in the health care field has been gaining support in response to increasing fiscal pressure and constraints. For the past 10 years, hospital utilization has been dropping steadily, leading to major reductions in programs and hospital consolidations and closures. This downward spiral is in direct response to changing reimbursement patterns (e.g., prospective-pricing systems and other types of fixed pricing systems), increased competition from other hospitals and alternative delivery systems (e.g., health maintenance organizations, managed care systems), and changing patterns of service delivery (e.g., the shift to ambulatory care, wellness programs) (Shaffer and Shaffer, 1988; Van Sumeren, 1986).

Many hospitals no longer operate within regional boundaries. National third-party payers are now seeking bids for services from hospitals across the country. Hospitals in Michigan no longer compete merely with each other; they may be competing with hospitals in Illinois, Kansas, and Ohio. The result has been decreasing bed utilization and increasing costs over revenue. Health care organizations are facing major changes in order to respond to the shrinking health care dollar, and the emphasis on reducing health care cost is not likely to disappear within the next decade.

Health care organizations have responded to this dismal financial picture through a variety of cost-saving strategies. Hospital closures and corporate mergers are becoming commonplace. Management consultants are being widely used to advise health care organizations how to cut costs in order to adapt to shrinking revenues. A common strategy for achieving cost-efficiency is to reduce staff.

This particular cost-saving strategy has been given different names: restructuring, downsizing, resizing, and right-sizing. Although there are subtle differences in these terms, managers and staff often describe the experience similarly as "cutbacks."

Downsizing is defined as an orderly process that has two facets: cost reduction and investment in new lines of business. Both steps are essential if downsizing is to result in a positive outcome (Shaffer and Shaffer, 1988; Maricich, 1985). In essence, it combines the microanalysis of staffing with a macroanalysis of the organization's structure and operations (Van Sumeren, 1986).

A myopic view of resizing strategies would be to focus solely on staff reductions to achieve cost efficiencies. The purpose of downsizing is to streamline staffing to an optimal level while maintaining high-quality service delivery (Van Sumeren, 1986). To cut staff without changing the way in which services are delivered could negatively impact the quality component of the equation. If the number of staff is reduced but the work is unchanged, the remaining staff will eventually burn out and the viability of the organization will be seriously threatened.

Effective resizing strategies are achieved not only through staff reductions but also by changing the way in which service is provided (Henkoff, 1990). The hardest challenge is freeing one's creative energy to critically examine the way in which services are delivered, to evaluate the skills necessary to perform the task, and to design and implement innovative strategies for reducing cost while maximizing quality.

Directors of social work and other human services departments are facing the need to respond to organizational mandates to reduce costs. There are several signs that trigger the need to downsize:

- Hospital occupancy rates are falling below acceptable levels.
- Cost of care is exceeding revenue.
- Organizational staffing levels (as measured in full-time equivalents) are increasing in spite of dropping profit margins.
- Consulting firms are being considered or have been scheduled to work with the hospital.
- There has been a change in organizational leadership and/or direction in which cost-efficiency becomes a priority.

Resizing Poses New Complexity

As these symptoms become evident, social work administrators need to begin preparing for potential resizing of their organizations. Hirschhorn (1983) suggests that the management of resizing poses new complexity for administrators in the following ways:

- Decision making regarding the allocation of resources becomes more difficult during resource decline.
- The political environment of the organization is more volatile.
- Retrenchment poses serious threats to mission and identity.

Decision-making complexity increases during times of resizing primarily in response to the deterioration or elimination of "slack" resources. Slack resources are the cushioning that allows for flexibility and enables managers to engage in creative and innovative ventures with less concern over success or failure. During times of retrenchment, the limited availability of slack resources makes the manager much more cautious. Errors or failures are much less tolerated, and a manager's credibility can be seriously damaged if the use of these resources is perceived as a mistake.

The unavailability of slack resources also contributes to a more politicized environment. When resources are abundant, conflicts often can be resolved by throwing additional resources to both of the conflicting parties. The conflict is achieved through a "win-win" solution. During times of resource decline, this method of conflict resolution often is not possible. Resources become limited, making it nearly impossible to address the needs of both conflicting parties. A "win-lose" environment for resource consumption is more prevalent. This "win-lose" environment increases competition and escalates organizational politics.

Finally, resizing can create serious disruption to organizational/departmental mission and identity. Under conditions of growth, systems are capable of expanding incrementally without changing core activities. The primary mission of the social work department may be to provide psychosocial care and discharge planning services for all inpatient units. During times of growth, the mission of the department may expand to incorporate ambulatory programs, such as outpatient clinics, hospice, home care, and substance abuse services while maintaining its original focus on inpatients.

During retrenchment, this expanded mission may come under scrutiny. With less staff to do the work, serious reexamination of priorities may be required. Is it better to provide services to all inpatients, or should resources be focused on specific programs? Should staffing from the ambulatory setting be pulled back in order to meet the original mission of servicing inpatients? Should the focus on outpatient services be maintained and inpatient services decreased because ambulatory settings are the wave of the future?

A reexamination of mission and identity is not necessarily a negative issue. Ongoing evaluation of the department's mission in relation to the context of today's world may be a necessary condition in a rapidly changing environment. McTighe (1979) suggests that it prevents many of the previously held high priorities, which may be outdated, from continuing to be performed at the expense of current high-priority needs.

Work redesign and restructuring can challenge cherished priorities, particularly regarding practices and beliefs about the role and function of social workers. Sacred models of supervision that stress the importance of supervisors carrying caseloads may be questioned (see chapter 3). Is it necessary to maintain an all-MSW staff? Can BSWs or clerical staff do some of the work done previously by MSWs and, if so, are we undercutting the profession? What exactly is social work's unique area of competence, its unique contribution to the organization? Each of these questions represents challenges to previously held beliefs about professional identity and role as social work practitioners in health care settings. These questions are not meant to be all-inclusive but merely to illustrate how issues related to departmental mission and professional identity are challenged during times of resource decline. Hirschhorn (1983, p. 2) sums up the dilemma as follows:

> Retrenchment planning creates a challenging new climate for decision making. Trade-offs are more severe, decisions hurt people, and interest groups and staff lose confidence in the criteria with which they evaluate alternatives.

Managing within this chaotic environment can feel overwhelming as social work administrators struggle to cope with the new complexity created by decision making during retrenchment. Resistance to change will be extremely high, increasing rigidity when flexibility is needed. Change is most easily accomplished when those affected have something to gain, but during times of decline, the acceptance of change will be unlikely because the rewards required to gain cooperation and build consensus are limited (Levine, 1979).

New Skills Are Needed to Manage Organizational Restructuring and Resizing

It is imperative that administrators develop skills to help them cope with the challenges of organizational decline. They must learn how to effectively manage within an environment characterized by uncertainty and emotional turmoil. They must become adept at the technical as well as the emotional aspects of the resizing process.

Think of your department as a boat navigating through waters infested with icebergs when a major storm hits. The waters become extremely choppy and steering the boat becomes difficult. Your chances of hitting an iceberg are greatly increasing. Although you continue to steer away from the icebergs, it becomes clear that a collision is inevitable. While you may no longer be able to avoid hitting an iceberg, you may have control over which iceberg you hit. An effective captain will have figured out which part of the boat can take a hit without sinking the ship. If a collision is truly unavoidable, then the captain will risk moving the ship toward the iceberg that will appear to do the least damage to the ship in order to avoid the ones that will clearly destroy the ship. If a collision must occur, the hope is to contain the damage so that the captain is able to keep the boat afloat until he/she is able to steer into safer waters. It is important to remember that any appearance of control may be significantly altered by the shape of the iceberg below the surface. If the captain is unable to predict or measure what exists below the surface, the iceberg can rip the ship in half without the captain having any warning.

This analogy is similar to the type of thinking that a manager must do when faced with downsizing. The manager may have no control over whether or not the organization reduces costs. Most organizations will deliver a cost-efficiency goal or mandate that departmental managers will have to achieve. Managers may only have control over where they take the cuts. An effective manager will make this decision based on where reductions will do the least amount of damage to the department for its present and future survival.

This ability to control the process may not always be possible. There are some situations where hospital administration will make decisions without involving departmental managers. The "iceberg below the surface" will determine the amount of damage. The only way to decrease the likelihood of this latter situation occurring is for the manager to begin adopting a mind-set toward reducing costs even if the organization has not. In this health care environment, achieving greater cost-efficiencies is inevitable and managers need to develop skills and strategies for dealing with retrenchment. However, this is not easy because most managers do not know how to manage during times of resource decline.

In order to achieve cost-efficiencies, management and staff must abandon old ways of thinking. The "old ways" of doing things were premised on models of organizational growth. Traditional organizational and management theories defined many of the problems to be solved by management action and organizational research (Levine, 1978) within environments of growth. Many of the top organizational administrators were schooled in methods premised on growth. For example, if hospital census is too high, expand the building to accommodate more beds; if acuity goes up, increase the number of staff. Levine suggests that the growth ideology has been so pervasive that it will require major shifts in management models and paradigms in order to function more effectively within environments characterized by decline.

There is little to guide the manager through models premised on retrenchment. Managers must approach this new environment with an openness to new ways of thinking. Henkoff (1990) refers to this as "paradigm busting." The manager of the future will be someone who embraces change and innovation. The following quote by Bridges (1988, p. 169) captures the mind-set needed:

> The skills necessary to turn change into personal opportunity begin with the ability to break free of the old way of seeing things and look at them in a new way. Ralph Waldo Emerson once said that if you don't believe that the world could look different, you need only bend over and look back at something through your legs. You need to run things upside down occasionally to stop seeing the pattern that you've imposed on them and let them take a new shape.
>
> What you need is illustrated in the story of the Zen patriarch who was deciding which of two students he ought to designate as his successor. The three of them meditated silently for several hours. Then, without warning, the patriarch took out a fan and handed it to one of them. The student looked surprised, but realized that he was supposed to do something with the fan, so he opened it, fanned himself a few times, and handed it back to the master. The latter passed it to the second student. The latter took it, opened it, fanned himself, closed it, and stuck it down the back of his collar where he used it as a back scratcher, then brought it out, opened it flat, put a cracker on it as thought it were a

> tray and held it out to the master. The master chose the latter as his successor.

Thriving in the present health care environment may depend on a manager's ability to think strategically and creatively about the delivery of social work services in health care organizations. When mandates to resize, right-size, or downsize are announced, the manager must be prepared to offer creative solutions that achieve cost-efficiency while preserving high-quality service delivery.

Resizing must be viewed within the context of change. According to Maricich (1985), downsizing involves a sequence of events in which each step prepares for the next step, but each step can also stand alone. The process of downsizing has been discussed by several authors (Bruce and Patterson, 1987; Maricich, 1985; Van Sumeren, 1986; Kazemek and Channon, 1988). It begins with analyzing the environment for change to establish expectations, conducting a diagnostic assessment of the organization in order to identify alternative strategies, and planning for implementation and evaluation.

This book will help managers wade through the multitude of decisions and strategies that will help determine the best place to take "the hit." Resizing must be viewed within the context of change. It is the context for change that shapes the structure of this book. Chapter 2 focuses on analyzing the organizational environment in order to set the context in which changes will take place. It represents the assessment phase of the change process. Chapters 3 and 4 explore the development of resizing strategies. Chapter 3 poses the critical questions a manager must address in order to develop a strategic plan for downsizing. Chapter 4 emphasizes the emotional component of downsizing and suggests strategies for managing this critical piece of the process. Chapter 5 focuses on issues related to implementation and evaluation of the downsizing strategy, with specific attention to the layoff process. Chapter 6 summarizes key issues discussed and encourages managers to engage in "paradigm busting" in order to face the future prepared to meet the challenges of an environment of fiscal constraint.

It is important that the reader recognize that the content of this book will serve only to help clarify the issues, decisions, and alternative strategies associated with the downsizing process. It is not meant to be a "cookbook" in the sense of describing a step-by-step guide to a specific outcome. The resizing process is situational. What works in one setting may not in another. To be effective, the manager must know how to "think" about the resizing process. Helping managers to do so is the purpose of this book.

Chapter 2

Planning for the Resizing Process

Examining the Environmental Context of Resizing and Restructuring

Whenever faced with a resizing or downsizing challenge, the social work administrator must consistently maintain a mind-set toward the broader organizational objectives. It is not only ineffective but also politically naive to engage in this process without a clear understanding of the environmental context within which this activity is to occur. For example, if hospital administration has identified "centers of excellence" or program priorities as part of their strategic plan, the social work manager would be unwise to target these same programs for reductions. Although this example may appear overly simplistic, it addresses a major error that many managers make when faced with downsizing.

There is often a tendency to begin by examining factors related to social work practice, for example: which workers are most productive, where is there the greatest support for social work services, or where is social work practice the most sophisticated. These factors should not be ignored, but they should not be the only measures against which decisions are made. For example, by eliminating a worker whose productivity is low, you may also eliminate or reduce services to a medical/surgical program. However, if this program is targeted by hospital administration for priority in resource allocation, the manager has weakened social work's position for growth unless the social work plan includes a reallocation of staffing to this program. By focusing on the organizational priorities, the decision to eliminate the worker with low productivity may not change, but the strategy will also involve transferring a more productive worker to this service area.

In order to develop an effective resizing strategy, the social work manager must understand the organizational or environmental context within which this change occurs. The ability of managers to accurately assess the external environment and to use this information in decision making is an essential element in organizational success (Johnson and Berger, 1990; Longest, 1981; Starkweather and Cook, 1988). This assessment process is the initial stage in any change activity.

The initial assessment phase of the change process uncovers the discrepancy between what is desired and what actually exists (Brager and Holloway, 1978). This information then serves as a basis for identifying strategies for intervention. The assessment process begins by collecting and organizing relevant data.

Getting the Information You Need

Managers must spend a sufficient amount of time seeking out a full range of information. This requires building a network of sources that covers a wide range of information. Management information systems (MISs), both in the department and the hospital, become a key resource in this process. Social work departments that do not have an adequate MIS, however, are not totally hindered. Many sources of information are a matter of record within the organization and can be divided into formal and informal categories.

Formal Sources of Information

Formal sources of information are defined as information in written format. These become formal because there is a "paper trail" to substantiate the information. The following is a list of some important formal sources of information within the organization:

- Statements of organizational mission
- Hospital budgets and other types of financial reports
- Personnel material (e.g., personnel practices, job descriptions)
- Hospital quality monitoring reports
- Admission, discharge, and length-of-stay data (by service if available)
- Strategic or five-year plans for the organization
- Minutes from the meetings of the hospital governing board or board of trustees

This list is not meant to be all-inclusive, but merely provides some examples of formal sources of information. Managers will need to identify additional sources specific to their own organizations. These formal sources of information are available but many are often ignored by managers. Minutes from board meetings may clarify organizational priorities and planning, familiarity with personnel policies will facilitate the layoff process, and budget reports will alert the manager to financial trends and problems that may have an impact on service delivery. The decision to downsize does not "suddenly" occur. Symptoms of the need for fiscal reductions are usually evident if one is looking for the signs.

Informal Sources of Information

Another important type of information is obtained from informal sources. These are defined as verbal exchanges or observations of behavior. Although more difficult to obtain, they are equally valuable to the decision-making process. Brager and Holloway (1978) listed the following sources of information that could be classified as informal:

- Observe meetings involving key decision makers as a way of gathering useful political information. Listen to what people do and don't say.
- Listen to the concerns, complaints, and aspirations of others.
- Determine the associations of key people both within and outside the organization.
- Learn about the prior behavior of key organizational participants.

Although these informal sources of information can be soft in terms of data, they often become useful tools when developing strategies for resource allocation. For example, a social work director was determining where to set priorities for the reallocation of staff after losing a full-time position through organizational downsizing. Two critical areas were being considered based on multiple sources of data substantiating the need for social work staff: inpatient psychiatry and the obstetrical clinic. Because staffing was not sufficient to cover both service needs, a decision had to be made as to which service would receive fewer social work resources.

At an administrative staff meeting, the CEO of the hospital discussed his concern about recent data on the poor infant mortality rate within the state. He ended the discussion by indicating that the hospital would develop a task force to develop strategies for improving service delivery to pregnant women (e.g., reduce waiting lists to the clinics, adding substance abuse counselors, etc.) The director of social work also learned that the CEO had recently been asked to serve on a statewide task force to focus on the problem of infant mortality. Given this information, the social work director decided to sustain social work staffing in the obstetrical clinic.

Information needs to continuously flow through social work administration so that the director or manager can make informed decisions in a timely fashion. If this attention to information only begins when a director or manager first learns of plans to resize the organization, it is too late. He or she will be forced to make decisions with little information to assess the short- and long-term implications of reducing resources.

Political-Economic Framework for Analyzing the Organizational Environment

Managers must continuously monitor the organizational environment in order to be informed about shifts and changes that are constantly occurring. In order to develop effective resizing strategies, a manager must know how to assess the environment in order to delineate factors critical to the decision-making process. An effective model for analyzing the context for change is to perform a political-economic analysis (Wamsly and Zald, 1973; Berger, 1990; Berger, 1982). This type of model is a useful approach for understanding why organizations develop and change over time. It views the organization from an open-systems perspective in which internal and external factors are equally relevant. The model postulates that there are two main structures in all organizations that shape behavior: the political structure and the economic structure. Each of these structures is examined both internally and externally to the organization to delineate patterns or interrelationships between variables that will shape the environment of decision making.

Figure 1: Political-Economic Framework

Environment Structure and Process	Internal Structure and Process
Political	***Political***
■ Subordinate and authoritative executive bodies and offices (and organized extensions—budget, personnel offices) ■ Superordinate and authoritative legislative bodies and committees (and organized extensions—ombudsman, inspectorates) ■ Independent review bodies—courts, judiciary ■ Competitors for jurisdiction and functions ■ Interest groups and political parties ■ Media-Communications entrepreneurs ■ Interested and potentially interested citizenry	■ Institutionalized distribution of authority and power Dominant coalitions or factions Opposition factions, etc. ■ Succession system for executive personnel ■ Recruitment and socialization system for executive cadre ■ Constitution Ethos, myths, norms, and values reflecting institutional purpose ■ Patters for aggregation and pressing demands for change by lower personnel
Economic	***Economic***
■ Input characteristics: labor, technology, facilities, supply, and cost factors ■ Output characteristics: demand characteristics and channels for registering demand ■ Industry structure (in and out of government) ■ Macro-economic effects on supply-demand characteristics	■ Allocation rules Accounting and information systems ■ Task and technology related unit differentiation ■ Incentive system Pay, promotion, tenure, and benefits ■ Authority structure for task accomplishment ■ Buffering technological or task core

Figure 1 delineates the variables associated with each of the structures (Wamsly and Zald, 1973). Because a thorough discussion of each of the criteria is not possible within the context of this book, readers are encouraged to read the work of Wamsly and Zald for a more detailed discussion. A discussion of each structure follows to demonstrate its relevance to resizing decisions.

Economic Structure

The economic structure refers to the system of production. It begins with importing resources into the organization, transforming them into services and/or goods, and disseminating them back into the community. *Economic* connotes factors of production, division of labor, allocation of resources for task accomplishment, and maximization of efficiency (Wamsly and Zald, 1973).

External economic structure

There are several good examples of how to utilize this model when looking at the external economic environment. For example, the explosion of new technology in the health care field is moving the delivery of health care services into the ambulatory areas. However, social work services are more likely to be concentrated on inpatient units. Given the priority for inpatient discharge planning, administrators may be inclined to reduce staffing in ambulatory areas. This may represent a short-term strategy that may have significant long-term consequences. Withdrawing resources from services that are likely to represent growth opportunities does not position social work to take advantage of these options. A manager might consider work redesign (see chapter 3) for discharge services in order to reduce costs on the inpatient side while preserving outpatient staffing.

Another factor is changing reimbursement patterns. Medicare, Medicaid (in some states), Aetna, and other purchasers of health care services are including social workers in their reimbursement schedules for outpatient services. Social workers are now able to bill for their services independently or through specific physician categories described as "incident to" physician services. Social workers can increase their ability to produce revenue for the organization rather than remain housed in the hospital's cost center.

The potential to generate revenue opens up a new set of strategies for resizing. An astute manager who recognizes the interrelationship between these two variables (i.e., increased care in ambulatory settings and social work's ability to bill for services) can approach downsizing with new alternatives. Rather than totally eliminate the ambulatory care workers, the strategic manager might move them from their cost center budgets to a newly created revenue budget, where expenses will be recovered through billing for social work services. By shifting the cost of staffing (including salary and benefits) from the cost center into a revenue center, one not only decreases the budget but also contributes to revenue enhancement for the hospital.

For example, in the state of Michigan, Crippled Children's has developed a program to provide comprehensive services for children (Comprehensive Multidisciplinary Clinics) in 22 specialty areas. This program offers dramatically larger reimbursement for the delivery of services. The availability of social work services was an eligibility requirement for every specialty clinic. At the University of Michigan Hospitals, one strategy for downsizing was to shift the cost of FTEs by recovering revenue generated in the clinics. The individual clinic will assume a portion of the cost for social work services by transferring dollars into the social work budget to cover the staffing cost and enable the personnel budget in the social work department to be decreased. The number of FTEs hasn't changed, only the funding source. This strategy enabled the department to reduce its budget while preserving the delivery of social work services to patients and the health care team.

Internal economic structure

Internal economic processes refer to the production cycle within the organization: how services are delivered and the mix of technology and personnel needed to deliver these services. As managers struggle to achieve organizational cost-efficiencies, they look for innovative, cost-effective strategies for providing similar or increased levels of care. Hence the phrase that has been striking fear into the hearts of managers for the past several years: "We need to do more with less." Although many are quick to interpret this to mean "working harder," it more appropriately asks for creative approaches for "working smarter." Most social work departments operate from austere budgets, but opportunities may still exist for improving operational efficiency. These questions need to be answered:

- Where are the inefficiencies within your department?
- Can social work services be delivered in a different way?
- Is there the right match between function and skill?

For example, the director of a department of social work began to question the efficiency of social workers arranging for equipment for patients being discharged from a rehabilitation unit. An analysis of tasks associated with the ordering of equipment documented the following concrete activities: gathering specific information regarding equipment needs from therapists (e.g., physical, occupational, respiratory therapists), ensuring that appropriate forms are completed, obtaining insurance verifications, identifying appropriate vendors, and ordering the equipment. This list is not to suggest that these are the only tasks associated with discharge planning, but it does delineate specific tasks that do not require a graduate education to complete.

After an evaluation of service delivery patterns, time requirements to order equipment, and cost to deliver these services, it was determined that a nonprofessional staff member (e.g., clerical staff) could assume responsibility for these specific tasks. A 50 percent reduction in cost was realized by hiring a clerical worker without compromising either the quantity or quality of services. The professional social work staff also experienced greater job satisfaction by directing their energy toward more sophisticated psychosocial clinical interventions.

A multitude of other examples are reported by social work directors across the country who have used similar strategies, including the following examples:

- Using centralized staff to communicate with nursing homes rather than having every staff member place his or her own initial and follow-up calls.
- Putting voice mail on each individual staff member's phone so that secretarial services required to take messages and for paging could be decreased.
- Implementing a computerized electronic mail system for staff in order to reduce the amount of secretarial time and resource consumption associated with the typing, photocopying, and phone time associated with communication functions.
- Developing internal backup systems with social work staff to provide vacation/sick leave coverage in order to reduce or eliminate monies set aside to pay for relief coverage.

Another example is associated with the increasing use of nurses. A more sophisticated system of nursing education combined with the nursing shortage (an example of an external economic factor) has led to a variety of changes in the health care system. Nurses are increasingly demanding higher salaries and more benefits. As the cost of nursing escalates, its widespread use is being called into question. Two examples will serve to illustrate this point.

On the inpatient psychiatric unit of a major teaching hospital, clinical nurse specialists were used to provide family treatment. Their intervention was limited totally to a therapeutic intervention with the family and did not include discharge planning. In addition, because the average length of stay had dramatically decreased to eight days, the question was raised as to the cost-efficiency of this program. Under the present arrangement, a family might be required to meet with the psychiatrist, the clinical nurse specialist, and the social worker, all within an eight-day stay. Social work management succeeded in convincing hospital administration that social work could not only provide the family intervention but also do so within the context of discharge planning and at a reduced cost (i.e., clinical nurse specialists earned on an average $5,000 more per year than social workers). This strategy not only provided a more cost-effective service leading to reduced hospital costs but also improved customer relations with patients and families.

The other example addresses the growing use of nurses to perform discharge planning. In some hospitals, social workers are being replaced by nurses to perform discharge planning as their sole function as opposed to floor nurses who facilitate discharge planning as part of their total patient care activity. As the cost of nursing services continues to increase, social work managers can position their department to regain this important function without getting into a "turf" battle. One need not question the appropriateness of nursing's involvement, only the cost-effectiveness. Inglehart (1990) studied 220 hospitals in California to evaluate the effectiveness of discharge planning services. A significant finding was that nurses were no more effective than social workers. If one accepts these findings, the significantly higher cost of nurses, combined with their limited availability in many areas would constitute a good argument for social work assuming greater responsibility for this function.

Some might question why social workers would even want to regain responsibility for discharge planning. Discharge planning has been regarded by some as "concrete" and of lower priority than more sophisticated interventions such as counseling. This attitude ignores the comprehensive scope of discharge planning in which helping patients and families adjust to the changes created by their illness and discharge plan is central to a successful outcome.

This attitude also ignores the critical importance of discharge planning within the economic and political structures of the hospital (Berger, 1990). Discharge planning is an essential component of the throughput process in the economic cycle. If patients are not discharged, beds are not available to admit new patients. Discharge delays can have a devastating impact on the hospital's financial picture within the present reimbursement system of prospective payment and, therefore, represents a point of critical uncertainty for the organization. Organizational influence will go to those individuals or departments who are able to cope with these uncertainties.

In all of these examples, strategies were implemented based on an assessment of internal and/or external economic factors. By examining the production cycle of the health care organization, both internally and externally, directors and managers can begin to gather essential economic information that can shape their decisions regarding resizing strategies.

Equally important to this process is a thorough assessment of the political structure. Although the economic and political structures are discussed as independent entities, they do not function independently. These two structures often interpenetrate and interrelate in such a way as to create a total organizational picture. What may appear to be economic may have a basis in the political structure. It is not so important to grasp the intricacies of the model, only that the two structures are interdependent and that an assessment of both is necessary to inform the manager of important trends and variables affecting the organization.

Political Structure

The political structure encompasses the systems of power, values for which power is used, and matters of legitimacy and distribution of power (Wamsly and Zald, 1973). The consideration of the political structure essentially requires a focus on issues of power.

External political structure

One can view the external political structure from two perspectives. First, there is the perspective of the department, from which the external environment would include the hospital administrators, CEO, board of trustees, chiefs of service, and consumers both within the hospital and the community. The other view would be from the perspective of the hospital. The external political environment would include the local government (e.g., city council), state government (e.g., governor, legislature), federal government (e.g., President, Congress, executive bodies), the courts, purchasers of health care, consumers, etc. The essential point is that the external political environment include those individuals or groups external to the system who hold some degree of influence over behavior within the system.

An example is the role of consulting firms. Hospitals contract with consulting firms to address critical organizational issues, including resizing and cost-efficiency programs. Their recommendations can often shape not only the process but also the outcome of organizational change. It is essential that the director or manager participate in the data collection process and learn as much as possible about the bias and strategies commonly employed by the consulting firm. Networking with colleagues in the Society for Hospital Social Work Directors or other hospitals to learn as much as possible about a specific firm can be critical to informing the strategy selected to deal with the consulting firm's organizational assessment.

A second strategy is to collect data that represent the departmental activity and the impact on the fiscal picture. Once again, the collection of data must represent an ongoing strategy because there is often insufficient time to collect and analyze the data once a consulting firm begins its work.

Social workers have used various other strategies to influence the environment for cost-efficiency planning. These include the following:

- Staying informed about legislation and rules that mandate the type and levels of service delivery
- Staying abreast of opportunities to influence purchasers of health care, particularly regarding billing for social work services, and demonstrating the cost-effectiveness of including coverage for social work
- Working within the political arena to develop and implement vendorship legislation

Although interventions focused at the external political environment often seem unrealistic or even idealistic given the increasing demands on management, the external environment should not be ignored. If that environment does not support policies and/or financing to promote health care services, the director/manager would be wise to begin planning for reductions well before the organization begins talking about it. The more time administrators have to prepare for and begin implementing cost-efficiency strategies, the greater the likelihood that their decisions will reflect strategies that sustain and possibly promote departmental growth in the future.

Internal political structure

Directors and managers are more likely to be attuned to the internal political environment of their organizations or departments than the external environments. Over the years, social workers have become astute in the art of organizational politics. They have shed their constraining view of politics as a "dirty word," something to be avoided.

As described in chapter 1, the downsizing/resizing process escalates organizational politics and moves it into a more volatile arena. To be successful, social workers must become even more adept at analyzing the internal political environment and employing strategies to influence decision making in a positive way (Berger, 1990).

It is essential for social work administrators and clinicians to become skilled politicians. This begins by identifying sources of power, developing a repertoire of strategies to influence change, and maintaining a "can do" attitude. These are challenging times with more than enough reasons to become recalcitrant or resistant to the constant onslaught of changes. In this health care environment, if you dig in your heels and refuse to change, the only thing you will get is two broken legs! This type of rigidity will often lead to the dismissal of the manager.

It is important to keep one's energy and attention focused on constructive solutions rather than on preserving the status quo. The question is no longer *should* there be change; the question is *how* to change. The successful implementation of resizing/downsizing programs will rest on the ability of directors and managers to assess the external environment and to use this information to influence the internal political environment. The following example illustrates this point.

A department of social work began planning for resizing and restructuring well in advance of any organizational announcement. Based on an assessment of both internal and external economic and political factors, the departmental administrators determined that reductions were imminent. When hospital administration called for reductions, the social work department was in the process of administrative restructuring in preparation for downsizing. Once hospital administration learned of the department's leadership, social work was held up as an example throughout the hospital of how to constructively approach cost-efficiency planning. When the second round of cuts was proposed, the social work department was excused. The departmental administrators strongly feel that this exemption was related to their constructive response to the first round of cuts as well as publicly supporting the "political elite."

A clear understanding of the power structures within the organization becomes critical to planning. If a strategy will have an impact on one of the "power players," careful planning and slow movement may be in order. A more thorough assessment of the environment for change may be needed and allies and adversaries identified. If the impact is likely to affect a person or an area that holds little power, implementation may be easier. If there is a choice, the strategy should be in the area that is less politically volatile.

The following are other critical strategies to use when dealing with the internal political environment:

- Pay attention to those individuals who are involved in the decision-making process.
- If consulting firms are utilized, find out who is meeting with the consultants.
- If strategic plans are developed, discover who is participating in this planning and which services have been identified as "centers of excellence" or slated for growth.
- Determine the allies of social work and their positions within the political structure. Consult with these individuals as planning unfolds.
- Position yourself within the organization as an individual who succeeds, even with limited resources.

This latter strategy is particularly important given current lean times. It comes back to maintaining an attitude of "can do." Hospital administration will be looking for individuals who can provide leadership. Developing a track record of success, particularly with limited resources, is likely to enhance future opportunities. A primary strategy in downsizing is to consolidate departments under one administrator, thus eliminating the other administrator positions. Hospital administration is likely to choose the individual most likely to be successful in leading this newly configured group, regardless of professional background. It is just as likely for social workers to take over utilization review, admitting, financial counseling, discharge planning, and pastoral care as it is for any other discipline. The common ingredient in this selection process is deciding who is the most qualified to get the job done.

Too often social work responds to these changes from a role of victimization. Hospital administration won't be looking for victims, but for leaders. In many ways, social workers may be the most qualified to assume these newly developed administrative positions. The decision will rest on the ability to influence the power structure of the organization in order to be positioned for new opportunities.

Social work directors and managers must embrace these changes, assume a position of helping the organization facilitate movement, and be willing to take risks. They must be able to accurately analyze the environment of change. The political-economic model provides an excellent tool to facilitate this analysis.

Chapter 3

Strategic Decision Making in the Resizing Process

Tough Choices and Hard Decisions

Cost-efficiency planning calls for creativity and innovation. A model that incorporates incremental change is often not useful within the rapidly changing environment of health care. Managers faced with implementing cost-efficiency plans are called upon to make tough decisions and hard choices. There is no simple solution or easy way to determine how to provide services at a reduced cost. There is no "cookbook" to tell one how to accomplish these difficult cost-efficiency goals.

This chapter explores issues and strategies that managers need to consider when faced with resizing or downsizing social work departments. The purpose is to highlight the issues that need to be explored by managers rather than prescribe a specific strategy. A number of examples are provided to illustrate the breadth of strategies available. However, these examples do not represent the totality of options.

It is important to understand that there is no *one* way to achieve cost-efficiency goals. Although commonalities exist, each manager's situation is unique. Departments, hospitals, and communities vary, calling for strategies specific to each situation. The primary objective of any manager is to engage in strategic decision making that maximizes opportunities while limiting the negative impact of downsizing/resizing. This involves hard decision making because managers are faced with a multitude of administrative dilemmas that compound the decision-making process.

Avoiding versus Smoothing the Impact of Cuts

Managers are faced with their first critical decision upon realizing that the hospital's financial picture is problematic. Their first decision focuses on whether to avoid cutbacks or to smooth their impact (Berger, 1991; Kazemek and Channon, 1988; Levine, 1979).

Avoidance strategies are based on the assumption that the financial problems are temporary setbacks and not critical. They attribute this swing to temporary decreases in patient volume, increased patient acuity, or the unique characteristics of service delivery in their organization. Arguments are composed as to why cuts are not possible; how reductions will significantly reduce the quality of services; or why there is not sufficient time to thoroughly analyze the situation and, therefore, an extension is needed before implementing a plan.

All of these can be described as delaying tactics or what Levine (1979) calls the "Tooth Fairy Syndrome." The manager believes that the cuts are not real or not necessary. Delaying managers believe that if they hold off cutting in their area, other managers will implement cuts within their departments, and then the delaying managers won't have to make cuts. By then, hospital administration will realize that further cuts won't be needed because the financial picture has improved. Behn (1980, p. 615) describes the phenomenon as follows: "We have little experience with contraction, and our psychological defense will work to convince us that, if we are only clever enough, retrenchment can be avoided (at least by us, if not by everyone." Although this position is understandable, to hold it without also exploring the possibility that cuts cannot be avoided is foolish.

Delaying tactics are premised on the idea that the financial crisis in health care is a short-term problem; if one waits long enough, the problem will go away. A thorough analysis of the present health care environment should suggest that these changes are not temporary. Indeed, we may only be seeing the tip of the iceberg in relationship to the need for dramatic changes in the way the health care field does business. Even if this country moves to some type of national health insurance, cost containment and the tight rationing of health care services will continue to be major driving forces. Delaying tactics are not likely to produce positive results. It is more likely that delaying the cuts may place not only the manager but also the department at risk.

A reason for delaying tactics is that the manager may not have been effectively analyzing the environment to identify indicators that reductions are imminent. These individuals often react with shock when they first hear that cost reductions are needed, layoffs may need to occur, or departmental consolidations are likely. Often the signs of these changes appear well before the formal announcement of change. For example, a declining profit margin or growing deficit, decreased admissions, an increasing percentage of contractuals in the payer mix, reductions in reimbursement from Medicare/Medicaid, and increases in the full-time equivalent (FTE) staffing ratios are a few such indicators.

Changes in organizational behavior can also be evident, such as tighter restrictions on travel, more stringent policies or controls for personnel recruitment, lower cost-of-living or merit increases in salaries, and possibly hiring freezes. This is where constant monitoring of the political-economic environment can ensure that the manager has adequate time to prepare strategies that address the need for change. These are all signs that more dramatic changes are coming and managers should begin planning.

Rather than adopting a delaying tactic, the manager would be wiser to explore strategies aimed at limiting the negative impact of the reductions. As a matter of practice, one manager develops the annual budget with projected budgetary decreases such as 2 or 5 percent when the hospital's financial picture is in decline. This encourages continuous thinking about where efficiencies could be achieved. By accepting that changes are inevitable and that cost reductions are essential to the survival of most health care organizations, managers are positioning themselves to explore strategies that will achieve long-term success for their departments by limiting the impact on the department's most important functions. Rather than expending energy on avoidance tactics, redirecting time and resources to incorporating cost-efficiency strategies into one's administrative repertoire may produce more advantageous results for the manager and the department of social work.

Energy should be directed toward exploring a variety of strategies to achieve cost-efficiency goals. One of the real challenges is to open one's thinking to new and different ways to deliver services. By focusing on strategies aimed at limiting the negative impact of cost reductions, managers allow for adequate planning to ensure the success of their decisions on present and future departmental functioning.

Short-Term versus Long-Term Implications of Resizing Strategies

A client once asked a consultant how to implement reductions so that the department could recover its losses in a short period of time. The consultant responded that the manager should begin by reframing his thinking. Rather than considering reductions as temporary, a manager needs to approach the problem from a perspective that these reductions are permanent. This latter perspective will direct one's thinking to long-term strategies, which are the roots of future growth because they must preserve social work's distinctive competencies.

As managers explore a multitude of strategies for resizing social work departments, they must constantly weigh the short-term versus long-term implications of each strategy. This tends to be challenging because the two are often inversely related. What has positive short-term effects can have disastrous long-term effects and vice versa. However, both perspectives are critical to the development of a balanced plan of action.

A short-term strategy may provide a quick solution and tend to focus on temporary or voluntary changes or solutions. Often these solutions offer ways to reduce budgets without permanent layoffs. Several of the following short-term strategies have been identified in the literature (Vestal, 1986; Lewis and Logalbo, 1980):

- *Wage and salary reductions.* Temporary reduction in wages for all workers or extension of the time period for awarding raises (e.g., from 12 months to 18 months).
- *Employee transfers.* Temporary transfer of a worker to an area that is understaffed (e.g., due to a vacancy).
- *Reduction of work hours.* Mandated time off without pay or working fewer hours per week.
- *Hiring freezes.* Leaving vacant positions unfilled.
- *Voluntary resignation.* Providing a fixed time during which a staff member can choose to voluntarily resign in exchange for a financial benefit.
- *Early retirement or retirement incentive.* Providing an incentive for employees nearing or at retirement age to voluntarily retire in exchange for a financial benefit.

One should evaluate short-term solutions with some caution. Short-term solutions, by definition, offer temporary solutions but may have negative long-term consequences if used as a permanent strategy. For example, a hiring freeze saves the money from salaries and benefits of vacant positions, but how long can an organization survive without filling vacancies? Voluntary resignations and early retirement reduce staff through voluntary departures and avoid layoffs, but this could create a "brain drain"; the most qualified staff may choose these options because they are most capable of finding another job. Also, retirees may cause the organization to lose a level of expertise that is critical to survival. Each of these strategies represents a viable solution, but if they are not viewed through a long-term lens, the outcomes for the long-term viability of the department could be disastrous. Vacancies and retirements do not always occur in areas where changes in service delivery would be targeted.

Such short-term strategies may be useful for identifying how the cuts will be achieved with minimal impact on existing staff but not where the changes in service delivery should be made. A long-term strategy will incorporate an analysis of patterns in service delivery and future anticipated growth for the organization. The remaining staff resources would then be reallocated to cover priority services identified through this analysis. This long-term strategy effectively positions social work for the future growth of the hospital.

Examples of long-term strategies include the following:

- *Reductions in the work force.* Layoffs of permanent staff.
- *Organizational restructuring.* Staff reductions in the administrative levels in the organization through flattening and consolidation.
- *Work redesign.* Redesigning the work process in order to eliminate barriers, rework, and unnecessary steps in the process, and to ensure a better fit between skill and function.

A more thorough discussion of layoffs is included in chapter 5, so discussion of long-term strategies will begin with organizational restructuring. There is a trend across American industry to de-layer, or flatten, organizational structures. Never before have the unemployment lines been filled by such a high number of white-collar workers. Probably the most vulnerable position in any organization, including health care, is the middle manager.

This trend is in response to changing philosophies and technology. With the explosion of information technology, much of the data regarding worker activity can now be captured on computerized management information systems and relevant information produced within a short turnaround time. Middle managers historically provided the link to this information. Upper management was kept informed by direct observation and reporting by middle managers. With information technology, this important and time-consuming function is no longer required, enabling further reductions of staff at these levels.

Another factor contributing to organization de-layering is the move to total quality management techniques within the Deming tradition. The whole premise of total quality management is to move decision making down the hierarchy so that problems can be solved at the lowest possible level. As responsibility and accountability move down the levels, the need for middle managers decreases. The move to self-managed teams within this model of management has also been a major factor in administrative reductions.

The move to flatten organizational structures has positive outcomes for the organization. Systems of communication greatly improve by decreasing the number of layers through which information must travel. Think about the children's game called "Telephone." A message is whispered in the ear of the first child in a chain. As each child whispers the message into the ear of the next child, the message becomes more and more distorted so that by the end of the chain, it is significantly different from the one in the beginning. This same phenomenon occurs in organizations. The more layers through which information must travel, the greater the distortion, as each person in the chain adds his or her own interpretation and understanding. By reducing the number of administrative layers, communication greatly improves in both quality and timing.

Another advantage of organization de-layering is that greater organizational flexibility is achieved. In hierarchical structure, more rigid boundaries become established between each discrete administrative unit. A manager's base of power becomes defined by his or her control over "turf." Change is more difficult because of the protective stance of managers over their domain. By reducing the boundaries, greater flexibility is achieved because a manager's span of control will be much more broadly defined. Often multiple units and services will be working together under one administrator, which promotes collaboration among these units.

Organizational flattening also carries negative consequences. One of the most striking is its effect on professional development. A key incentive for motivating staff is the prospect of career advancement. In a flattened departmental structure, there are fewer promotional opportunities. This is an important issue to consider when developing strategies for dealing with those staff who remain after the layoffs (refer to the discussion of "survivors" in chapter 5).

Administrative restructuring works in tandem with work redesign. The premise of work redesign is to restructure the work to eliminate barriers to efficiency and to achieve the best fit between skills and function. Administrative restructuring is a type of work redesign where the work of managers and administrators is altered.

An additional example of work redesign at the administrative level touches upon a "sacred cow" in professional circles. Professionals hold that managers of clinical services should carry a clinical caseload as part of their normal responsibility. This clinical responsibility may range from 10 to 75 percent depending on the organization. The clinical assignment includes coverage of a defined clinic or inpatient unit, usually a specialty area. It is time to reexamine the efficiency of this model.

From a fiscal point of view, is it cost-effective? If a manager pays supervisors $35,000 and line workers $25,000, why should the higher salary be paid for work that could be performed by a worker at a lower salary? Why not restrict the supervisor's activities to those functions that cannot be performed by the line worker? This would allow a reduction in the number of supervisors and move clinical services back into the line at a less expensive rate.

If a manager believes that supervisors can't be effective unless they keep their fingers in clinical work, then let the supervisors achieve this by backing up their line workers. This may be an even better approach. The supervisors will have direct experience on the worker's service, enabling supervisors to provide better coaching because they can draw upon their own knowledge of the service.

Another advantage is decreasing role conflict. Many line supervisors report difficulty in constantly having to shift between clinical and supervisor roles. One minute the supervisor is a clinical peer and the next a manager. Not only does this create tension for the supervisor but often contributes to slippage in productivity as the supervisor shifts back and forth between roles.

Another example of work redesign is the introduction of staff who do not hold graduate degrees. As resources begin to shrink, departments of social work are looking at "social work extenders," "social work assistants," and "social work technicians" to perform some of the duties presently performed by MSW staff. Some may perceive this as a denigration of the MSW, but it may in reality be an elevation of this role.

It is difficult to believe that arranging transportation, getting clothes from a shelter in order to discharge a patient, or completing forms requires a graduate education. These tasks often take away time for functions that do require professional skills such as psychosocial assessments, clinical intervention with patients and families, patient education, and group work.

The challenge of downsizing is to reduce costs without compromising quality of service. Work redesign is one strategy that may allow the manager to reduce costs without significantly altering the number of staff. An example may help to demonstrate how this can be accomplished.

A department of social work was required to eliminate a 0.50 FTE at the clinical social work level (about $15,000). After conducting a thorough evaluation of internal and external factors, the decision was made to achieve this goal on the cancer service. An analysis of staff activity on this service revealed that each of the two social workers (2.0 MSW FTEs) in radiation oncology spent about 65 percent of their time performing concrete tasks (e.g., arranging transportation and housing). The director decided to transfer one of the MSWs to a vacant position on another service and to hire a 1.0 FTE "social work technician." The MSW who was transferred was paid $32,000 per year. The social work technician received $17,000 per year. The radiation oncology service continued to function with 2.0 FTEs but tasks were now divided with the technician handling all transportation and housing activity and the MSW performing all the psychosocial assessments, counseling, and other clinical activity. The goal of saving $15,000 was achieved by redesigning the work rather than merely eliminating an FTE.

One technique for generating creativity with work redesign is to engage in "zero-based staffing." Take the personalities out of the position and behave as if you have just received a sum of money to staff a new social work department. Begin by identifying service priorities. Then look closely at what level of skills is needed to achieve service goals. Can some of the more concrete services be handled by a technician or secretary? Can BSW staff be used in new and creative ways? Can functions be consolidated to reduce complexity in service delivery? Do you need the same number of supervisors? Can supervision be handled differently?

One of the biggest barriers to thinking creatively is the reality that there are people in these positions. These people have been our colleagues and our friends. These people have wishes and desires about how they would like to practice or how services should be delivered. These people have families who depend on their income or are self-supporting. The manager must separate the emotional component. This does not suggest that the emotional content be ignored, but it can't become the dominant factor in decisions regarding resizing and restructuring departments.

It is critical that the manager weigh the pros and cons of short-term strategies carefully. Another example illustrates the delicate tension between short-term and long-term approaches. A major teaching hospital was faced with implementing a 7 percent cost reduction. After an analysis of external and internal political and economic factors, the department managers decided to make the cuts in psychiatric services. The psychiatry program had 2.0 FTEs at the MSW level and 1.0 FTE atthe BSW level. The medical and nursing staff had been critical of the MSWs but were supportive of the BSW because this individual was responsible for discharge planning. The two MSWs worked with two clinical nurse specialists in the family therapy program. The MSW role was defined exclusively as providing family therapy. The social work department managers were dissatisfied with this limited definition of the MSW role but faced significant resistance from the MSWs when efforts were made to redefine it.

A short-term solution would have been to eliminate one of the MSW positions. This would have netted more dollars toward cost reductions and would also have eliminated an employee who was resistant to change. The health care team would also have been supportive of this strategy. It sounds like a good solution, but let's reexamine the long-term implications.

By eliminating an MSW, the basic pattern of service delivery would go unchanged. The MSW would continue to provide family therapy and the BSW discharge planning services. This conveys a message that discharge planning is only a technical process involving concrete services, rather than a clinical issue that involves clinical interventions with patients and families to accomplish discharge goals. It also perpetuates the dichotomy that work with families is somehow separate and distinct from the discharge planning process.

The environmental analysis also documented that the length of stay on the psychiatry units had been greatly reduced over the past year from an average of 30 days to 8 days. Shorter lengths of stay called into question the efficacy of providing family therapy on this inpatient unit. During an eight-day stay, under the present system, the patient's family would meet with the physician at least once, the BSW for discharge planning, and the family therapist. A redefinition of the role of "family work" was needed, emphasizing its importance in the process of assessment and discharge planning. To accomplish this, an MSW was needed to incorporate both functions: family work and discharge planning.

The analysis indicated that although the short-term solution would net the most money and positive staff support, the long-term implications would have eroded social work's basic competency and critically hindered its future in psychiatry services. The decision was made to eliminate the BSW position and redefine the role of the two MSWs to include discharge planning. Two years after implementing this decision, social work services expanded. The family therapy program was eliminated and one of the clinical nurse specialist positions assigned to this program was converted to an MSW position.

The Values, Norms, and Policies that Shape the Decision-Making Process

The organizational culture and personnel policies often become guiding principles when approaching the resizing process. Because resizing strategies often lead to changes in roles and/or elimination of positions, it is important that managers clearly delineate the values, norms, and personnel policies that will shape the process.

One of the first things a manager should do is become acquainted with personnel policies governing changes in employment or job descriptions. These policies often define the boundaries in which staff changes occur. The following questions need to be addressed:

- Is there a system of seniority operating within the personnel structure? If so, are there any exceptions to this policy?
- Is there bumping within the system (i.e., an employee claiming the position of a less senior employee)?
- What are the guidelines for implementing layoffs?
- Is there training for managers as to how to conduct layoff interviews?
- What are the manager's and employee's rights in relation to changes in an employee's hours, both increases and decreases?
- What are the manager's and employee's rights in relation to changes in an employee's job function?

As much as a manager thinks he or she knows personnel policies, working with reductions in staff poses a new set of dilemmas that most managers have not experienced. To be effective, a manager must clearly understand how personnel policies are implemented in relation to staff reductions. A manager should not be afraid to involve the personnel office if necessary to get answers to critical questions.

Any deviation from personnel practices may land the manager in an unnecessary grievance action and/or litigation.

In addition, managers must take the time to identify the values and norms that will shape strategies for resizing their departments. How will information be handled and what role will the staff play in the communication of information and decision making? How does one's right to dignity and self-determination shape decisions regarding staff participation? Staffs' and managers' confidence in the process increase if they feel that decisions will be guided by a strong ethical base (Johnson and Berger, 1990; Berger, 1991).

Across-the-Board Cuts versus Targeted Cuts

A pivotal decision regarding resizing rests with a determination of the rules for allocating the cuts. This usually involves a tradeoff between equity and efficiency. Levine (1978, p. 320) defines equity as "the distribution of cuts across the organization with an equal probability of hurting all units and employees irrespective of impacts on the long-term capacity of the organization" and efficiency as "the sorting, sifting, and assignment of cuts to those people and units in the organization so that for a given budget decrement, cuts are allocated to minimize the long-term loss in total benefits to the organization as a whole, irrespective of their distribution." Deciding where to make the cuts is one of the most difficult decisions a manager must make. There is no easy choice since both equity and efficiency have their strengths and weaknesses.

There is a tendency among social work managers to search for strategies that are characterized by "fairness" (Berger, 1991). All too often "fairness" is elusive and strategies that appear to be fair may actually negatively impact others. For example, seniority policies are often considered fair because they apply objective criteria to decision making. However, seniority often negatively impacts minorities because they are often the most recently hired employees.

Across-the-board cuts are also categorized as fair because everyone equally shares in the reduction. According to Turem and Born (1983, p. 206), "This across-the-board, 'share and share alike' approach to retrenchment is probably the most ideologically palatable alternative for human service professionals, many of whom . . . subscribe to what has been called the 'ethic of goodness.'" Across-the-board cuts may appear fair, but in reality, could produce long-range consequences that could hurt all staff and lead to the eventual demise of the department.

Across-the-board cuts assume that all parts of the department are equal and that if everyone assumes a small reduction in time, it will have the least negative impact on staff and patient care. However, the opposite effect may occur.

For example, staff members agree to reduce their workday to 75 percent time so that no one loses his position. To implement this, staff agree to work from 9:00 a.m. to 4:00 p.m. instead of from 8:00 a.m. to 5:00 p.m. With this type of arrangement, staff will be expected to do the same amount of work in less time because no programmatic changes were implemented. Staff will increasingly feel overworked and "burned out." This negatively affects staff morale, which in turn decreases productivity. If productivity declines, the department is placed in a more vulnerable position should an additional round of cuts occur.

Across-the-board cuts also ignore organizational priorities. They assume that the present ranking of priorities will be the same in the future. In reality, hospitals are moving more toward identifying "centers of excellence" as they compete for market share. They have come to realize that they cannot provide all services to everyone and still compete within the market. Hospitals are now targeting programs for priority in resource allocation. If social work departments implement cuts across-the-board, they may jeopardize their position in relation to these priorities.

Finally, across-the-board cuts have been described as short-term strategies or delaying tactics (Behn, 1980, "Leadership . . ."; Lewis and Logalbo, 1980). They presume that the reductions are only temporary and, therefore, do not require major alterations to organizational priorities and practices. Although an across-the-board approach may be effective under minor and/or temporary conditions, it will not position the organization for future success if employed when permanent solutions are required.

A more responsible managerial decision is to target the cuts through programmatic changes. These targeted cuts should be made to programs or services that have the least impact on the department's distinctive competence within the organization. In the example above regarding the inpatient psychiatry program, the departmental administrators targeted the cuts to withdraw from a purely psychotherapeutic service (i.e., family therapy) to a more traditional model of practice that included psychosocial assessments, discharge planning, and counseling.

The Role of Staff in Decision Making for Resizing Strategies

There is little agreement in the literature regarding the level of staff participation in the resizing process. Opinions vary across a wide continuum from no participation to total participation. There is no clear-cut answer to this dilemma because managers will stand up and recount horrible examples as a result of each approach. Chapter 5 discusses the importance of participation in the layoff process, but the issue has broader implications for the entire process of resizing.

Opponents of disclosure will point to the increased resistance related to staff's anxiety about the uncertainty of their futures. Employees will draw into a defensive posture, unwilling to engage in an exploration of alternative strategies for downsizing, and possibly sabotage these efforts. As staff morale plummets, departmental productivity declines, placing the department at greater risk for future reductions.

The answer to this dilemma may lie in the historical roots of the profession, which believes in an individual's right to self-determination. In order to make informed decisions, individuals have the right to know how factors within the organizational environment may affect their futures. Workers have a right to know if their jobs are at risk or their positions within the organization are in jeopardy. This allows individuals to make responsible decisions regarding their future, regaining some control over their own fate.

Proponents of participation will point out that increased participation encourages change. The destructive aspect of rumors is limited by open sharing of information, and participation inhibits the development of a "we" versus "they" orientation to survival. The more people engage in the planning process for the future by clarifying their own options, strengths, and decisions, the more they will be willing and able to help design a program to which they might not belong or one in which their roles will be different (Berger, 1991; Johnson and Berger, 1990; Hirschhorn, 1983; Levine, 1979). An example may help to illustrate these advantages.

A director of a large department of social work in an urban, tertiary care hospital predicted from several financial indicators that the hospital would be facing serious downsizing. These suspicions were validated when the hospital hired a consultant to specifically evaluate the management structure of the entire hospital, including at the departmental level. The director met with her management team to alert them to her growing concern. In this meeting she emphasized that no one sitting in this meeting had any job security, including the director. She would not promise any of them that they would hold a management position by the end of one year or a job if their seniority was low. She encouraged each of them to begin exploring other options and committed her support and assistance to them.

Throughout the year, these managers actively participated in planning for a future to which they might not belong. They explored a variety of options for reducing costs even though there had been no mandate from hospital administration to do so. Although the process was at times difficult, they were able to free up their energies to address the resizing plan because their own futures were clarified and placed back into their control by allowing and encouraging them to explore alternatives. This is not to say that the managers welcomed the changes or did not suffer emotionally. It does suggest that they were provided sufficient information to begin making decisions about their own future in areas over which they had some control. It is interesting to note that by the time the hospital implemented the downsizing mandate, four of the eight managers and supervisors had located jobs outside of the organization that offered promotional opportunity or increased pay.

Advanced Notification of Layoffs and Personnel Changes

One of the most critical decisions a manager must make is when to inform staff of major changes that will have a significant impact on their positions. There is debate among managers and personnel representatives about what is a sufficient amount of notice. The continuum ranges from immediate departure upon notification to an indefinite period of time. Each approach comes with a plausible rationale and a variety of success and horror stories. This issue of when to share information can be one of the most anxiety-producing aspects of the process and should be thoroughly evaluated (see chapter 5 for a more complete discussion of this issue).

Hirschhorn (1983, p. 24) states: "A manager's capacity for leadership is severely tested when he or she must decide whether or not to reveal bad news to the staff." At one extreme, the manager fears that staff will panic or become hostile, disrupting the work environment and creating new management headaches. At the other extreme, if a manager withholds information, anxiety due to the uncertainty of the situation will increase, rumors will replace missing information, and the manager's credibility will be seriously damaged.

It is important that the reader understand the bias of the author. I encourage early notification of staff so that they have sufficient time to plan for their future. Too often, the withholding of information is in direct relationship to the manager's discomfort in dealing with conflict. Proponents of "no notice," dismissing the employee immediately upon notification, have adopted models utilized in the business world. These models speak to concerns over espionage, sabotage, and disruptions to the workplace. It is hard to imagine what deep, dark secrets are held by the social work department that would warrant these fears. The concern over disruption, whether intentional or not, is fundamentally a concern over a manager's ability to manage during times of conflict.

The issue may be not *when* to inform but *how* to inform. If the manager merely provides the information as factual but has not clearly thought through the ramifications of notification, one should anticipate conflict of a major proportion. Managers must clearly examine not only when to tell employees but also how and when to inform others on the health care team about the changes. A clear plan of communication across the organization must be developed so that information and not rumor is disseminated. If the flow of information is not managed correctly, the likelihood and intensity of disruption will increase.

For example, a hospital had discharge planning services lodged in a separate department staffed by a highly expensive, experienced BSN staff. As part of the organizational cost-efficiency plan, hospital administration decided to eliminate the department and have discharge planning services absorbed by social work and nursing. The director of nursing and the director of social work were asked to chair a task force to develop a plan for absorbing discharge planning functions. Hospital administrators met with the discharge planning department to inform them of this decision, giving them six months advance notice so that they could obtain other positions. There was no organized plan for dissemination of this decision to all hospital personnel. By the end of the day, floor nurses, physicians, vendors, and community agencies were calling to complain. The rumors included: discharge planning services were being eliminated, physicians would have to do their own arrangements for discharge planning, floor nursing would assume responsibility for all discharge planning services, and social work was assuming all responsibility for discharge planning services. This latter rumor brought in the nursing union, which claimed nursing functions would be performed by nonnurses in direct violation of the contract. The issue became so emotionally and politically volatile that the decision was almost withdrawn. Even when administration held its course, the process of transition was seriously hindered by the volatile environment.

Management's immediate response was to point to this event as evidence that early notification was bad. The problems may not lie with the timing but with the *process* of communicating information. Any decision of this magnitude would have evoked strong reaction. Had appropriate and factual information been disseminated, much of the concern and misinformation could have been prevented. Although it might not have eliminated opposition, it would certainly have decreased the scope and intensity of the conflict.

The previous example where the director informed her management staff of administrative restructuring one year prior to its implementation supports early notification. The management staff were able not only to find alternative employment but also to engage in departmental planning for change despite knowing that they may not have a management position within the new structure.

As stated earlier, there is no clear direction on this issue. Each manager will need to evaluate this issue very carefully, in conjunction with personnel policies and procedures. This author concurs with Hirschhorn's (1983) three maxims regarding disclosure of information (p. 28):

1. It is better to disclose too much than too little.
2. It is better to disclose too early than too late.
3. It is better to disclose too much to the inside at the risk of disclosing too much to the outside.

Chapter 4

Managing the Emotional Context of Resizing

Change in its most positive form would not be described as an easy process. People and organizations are reluctant to change, to give up the familiar, even if they know that the present state of affairs is unpleasant or harmful. Resizing in its purest form is nothing more than an organizational change process aimed at reducing organizational costs without compromising quality.

Resizing has the added burden that most employees will not perceive this process as positive. This increases when management has not provided adequate information to staff about the deteriorating financial picture. Their own feelings of incompetence and failure, denial about the seriousness or permanence of the situation, and fear that this negative information will leak to the community and further jeopardize their position may encourage administrators to shield staff from this distressing information.

Even when management has done an excellent job of keeping staff informed, resistance to this change process should be expected because it represents significant loss. It could mean loss of job, loss of friends and co-workers, loss of routine, and loss of status, to name a few. Bridges (1988) identifies six categories of loss experienced by employees: loss of attachment, turf, structure, future, meaning, and control. It is this overwhelming sense of loss that produces the significant emotions that can have a deleterious effect if not managed effectively.

Managing the emotional context of resizing can be one of the greatest challenges of a manager. Hirschhorn (1983) found that patterns of denial, anxiety, and the balance between pessimism and optimism can shape the framework for rational decision making. An additional factor escalating the emotional chaos is the chronic uncertainty that characterizes the resizing process. This chapter examines the emotional context of change associated with the resizing process and some strategies managers can employ. Once again, these strategies are not prescriptive but only serve as ideas and suggestions for how to effectively manage this component of the process.

Denial: A Destructive or Constructive Reaction

Denial is one of the most common reactions. It is a common defense mechanism for coping with crisis and is not necessarily detrimental. Managers and staff often need to deny the deeper meaning of resizing in order to continue to function in their present jobs. They cannot continue to perform their duties effectively if their thoughts are constantly bombarded by threats to their personal security. Will I be demoted or, worse yet, lose my job? How much will my salary be reduced? How long before I get my pink slip (refer to chapters 3 and 5 for a more detailed discussion of job loss fear)? Maslow's theory of "hierarchy of need" pointed out that individuals are not able to deal with the more complex psychological tasks if their basic needs for survival are in jeopardy. We have no hope of engaging staff in the process and drawing upon their creativity and job knowledge unless they have first come to terms with their own job security. Therefore, it is critical that managers convey as much information as possible, so that staff can continuously assess their own issues of job security, and encourage them to actively explore options.

Denial can be counterproductive if it inhibits an individual's ability to engage in the change process. As pointed out in chapter 3, denial is a major factor contributing to management's selection of strategies. It can produce avoidance of the cuts or selection of short-term solutions because decision makers deny the long-term reality of the need for change. Staff denial will manifest in an unwillingness or inability to explore alternatives and options for delivering services differently. They may resist opportunities for new employment because they do not believe their jobs will be affected.

A poignant example of denial is when staff do not believe that their work will change in light of staff reductions. They believe that a 10 or 20 percent reduction in budgets will not change the way they do business. They acknowledge that other staff have lost their jobs or that there may be less money for supplies or travel, but as long as they didn't lose their jobs, it will be business as usual.

Managing Anxiety

Another challenge in managing the emotional context is dealing with anxiety. There are times when the manager may wish the staff would engage in *more* denial in order to avoid the constant battering associated with anxiety. Free-floating anxiety can be extremely incapacitating and disruptive to the work environment unless managed effectively. One cannot eliminate anxiety any more than one can eliminate denial. It is an inherent aspect of the change process. The challenge is to manage it so that staff members have an outlet for their fears and emotional turmoil without overwhelming the organization's ability to function.

Strategies for Managing the Emotional Content of Resizing

Hirschhorn (1983) identifies the following five key strategies for managing the emotional content:

- Legitimize the emotional dimension.
- Project a willingness to be both active and passive.
- Find a balance between optimism and pessimism.
- Develop adequate support for the emotional content of management.
- Reduce anxiety through effective management of organizational uncertainty.

Strategy 1: Legitimize the Emotional Dimension

Legitimizing the emotional dimension begins by acknowledging that it exists. It is not uncommon for managers to shut off this piece of the reality because of their inability to deal with their own emotions. Managers are always called upon to make tough decisions, many of which negatively affect others. They often build up protective walls to shut off the emotional component, which may impede their ability to make such decisions. This becomes incorporated into their style and demeanor. Others begin to feel that these managers don't care because they do not display behavior that signifies the reality of the emotional turmoil, or they avoid any discussion of feelings, either their own or their staff's.

An example may help to illustrate. A director of a department of social work had spent several staff meetings talking about the need for resizing due to fiscal decline. The director felt strongly about sharing the facts with staff so that they could be informed and plan for their future. The director often shared his regret for the need to downsize. The director sought consultation in order to more effectively manage the growing problem with staff morale and resistance to planning for alternative delivery systems. Feedback from staff indicated that they felt the director was insensitive to the impact of these changes on staff. The director was shocked when he heard this, feeling that he had in fact acknowledged their feelings. He described sleepless nights and frustration over having to implement downsizing strategies because of the negative impact it would have on staff.

After careful exploration, the manager came to realize that his demeanor communicated lack of emotion. He communicated difficult information in a "matter-of-fact" tone and avoided any discussion of how staff felt about the news. He avoided these discussions because of his own fear that he would "lose control." With the consultant's help, the director devoted a block of time at the next series of staff meetings to discuss staff concerns and feelings about the impending changes. The director also shared with staff some of his own feelings. By the last staff meeting, the staff began talking about some alternative ways to deliver services and decided to break up into work groups in order to begin looking at several alternatives.

During times of retrenchment, managers must make an extra effort to acknowledge not only the emotions of their staff but also their own conflicts. The manager must create a climate where staff are encouraged to deal with their feelings. Adequate time, space, and resources (e.g., facilitators, employee assistance personnel) should be made available to staff. It may not be necessary to schedule special formal meetings to do this work (e.g., sensitivity groups), though these can be employed. Encouraging these activities within existing staff or work groups can be equally effective. The important element is that feelings are recognized and allowed to air, or else the other more technical work of change cannot take place.

Strategy 2: Be Both Active and Passive

Strategy 2 focuses on the manager's ability to project an atmosphere of realism. It is important that the manager convey a willingness to be both active and passive in his or her approach in response to the reality of the situation. Directors should adopt active strategies when they have the ability to shape opportunities, and passive strategies when opposition would be counterproductive based on the strength of external forces. Inappropriate activism or passivity will erode the director's credibility, leaving staff feeling more anxious because of a leadership vacuum.

Inappropriate activism is a common response of managers, particularly if they adopt a belief that the impending changes would be due to their inadequacy as a manager. These managers assume a posture that communicates that they can accomplish whatever they set out to do. They can avoid having to reduce staff; they can stop administration from reducing the department's budget; they can keep others from taking over social work office space. Hirschhorn (1983) describes this as "dare to be great" posturing. Unless managers are capable of stopping these universal forces of change from occurring, they would be wise to present a more realistic picture. They can present their position as departmental goals but also infuse the reality that, given the fiscal conditions of the organization, they may not be achievable. Managers often adopt this type of posturing because they believe it improves departmental morale. However, unless managers can deliver on these promises, it will only destroy morale as staff lose faith in their leadership.

A small community-based hospital proposed a 5 percent reduction in costs. The director of social work reported that she had spent a significant amount of time collecting data to substantiate why cuts to the department were not possible. At staff meetings, she reassured staff that the department would not sustain any reductions because of the essential nature of their work to patients. The director's entire strategy was based on preventing the cuts and assumed this position publicly. The director reported being "shocked" to learn that her position had been eliminated and the department placed under the department of utilization review.

In this example, the director's activism was inappropriate. She behaved as if the cuts would not affect her or her department. A more appropriate strategy may have been to accept that cuts were inevitable and develop strategies that would have achieved these reductions within her department or propose consolidations of other departments under the social work department. Another example may be useful to illustrate the impact of inappropriate activism.

The emergency department was undergoing major changes as part of a cost-efficiency program. Office space became a key issue in the discussions. The medical director of the emergency department arbitrarily assigned clinical nurse specialists to share space occupied by social work. The director of social work visited the emergency room and declared to her staff that in one week, the nurses would be moved. After several weeks, no changes in space allocations were made and the director of social work did not visit the staff to explain why. The result was that the director's credibility was damaged. This presented significant concern for the social work staff in light of the cost reductions being proposed for the emergency department. The social work staff began looking for and accepting positions in other hospitals because they no longer felt the director could protect them from the negative components of the change process. With the social work program in the emergency department weakened by staff openings, the position of the department was compromised.

In both of these examples, inappropriate activism led to problems that could have been prevented. The solution is not to assume a purely passive stance to change, but to be realistic and avoid making promises that may not be possible to keep.

Inappropriate passivity is equally detrimental. This is more commonly manifested in posturing associated with "victimization." For example, a hospital implemented a major cost-efficiency program characterized by significant restructuring of hospital departments and services. Throughout the process, the director of social work would communicate any changes associated with the department as "hospital administration required me . . . ." At no time did the director own any responsibility for departmental changes through either agreement with the direction of the hospital or ownership of the direction of internal changes. The director portrayed herself as a "victim" to the whims of an evil administration.

As a result, the staff began to display behavior associated with powerlessness. They described their own feelings of victimization. Staff anxiety escalated and morale plunged. Absenteeism and low productivity began to appear. Rumors were running rampant and everyone assumed a vigilant protective stance over what they defined as their "turf." The director's ability to achieve constructive change was nearly impossible, and the position of the department within the organization was seriously jeopardized.

To offset excessive passivity or activism, the manager must maintain a realistic picture of organizational events and changes. Managers are most credible when they can acknowledge the significance of environmental or organizational constraints while at the same time projecting a "can do" attitude in those areas where barriers can be overcome. This "can do" attitude can be achieved by actively seeking out relevant information rather than waiting for someone to provide it, developing effective coalitions, and utilizing political skills to change those areas that are capable of being changed. When managers fail to communicate a realistic picture, their credibility may be seriously damaged. This will only lead to greater problems with staff morale, increased confusion among staff, and escalating anxiety.

Strategy 3: Balance Optimism and Pessimism

The third strategy calls for a balance in optimism and pessimism. It is similar to the second strategy in that it deals with projecting a realistic picture of the situation. Extremes in optimism and pessimism can produce results similar to extremes in activism and passivity. If a manager projects an overly optimistic attitude, it may force staff to drive their anxiety underground through the rumor mill. As with any conflict that goes underground, it often festers and grows until it resurfaces in a much more destructive way. If a "disaster" does hit the department, the manager's credibility may be permanently damaged, and the staff may perceive their situation to be leaderless. A manager who is too pessimistic may create a climate where no constructive action can be imagined, leaving a feeling of powerlessness in its wake.

It is important to discuss the role of rumors. Rumors are an important form of communication and an information mechanism that can be beneficial to planning if harnessed constructively. They can also be destructive if they become the primary means for information dissemination.

To channel the constructive elements of rumors, one strategy a manager might employ is to begin staff meetings with "rumor control." A key element to rumor control is that the person does not have to own the question or information. In that way, staff are more likely to ask questions or seek information that they might not be willing to risk asking for fear of exposure. This strategy has several advantages for managers. It becomes an important deterrent to information going underground where the manager loses control over it. Also, it becomes a significant source of organizationwide information through your staff's broad networks.

Strategy 4: Adequately Support the Emotional Content of Management

The fourth strategy to managing the emotional dimension of the resizing process is for managers to develop effective support mechanisms for themselves. Traditional mechanisms may not always be effective, particularly if the support system consists solely of organizational peers. Organizational retrenchment can foster competitiveness as change takes on an increasingly "win-lose" definition. One's ability to obtain support may also be hampered by colleagues' lack of experience and familiarity with resizing. There is also a wish to avoid these discussions as others may try to hide from the reality.

It is imperative that the managers seek out effective support systems during this process of change. Managers' leadership skills will be significantly tested as they attempt to maintain staff commitment while significantly changing staff's lives. Suddenly the weight of responsibility seems overwhelming. The burden of making decisions that could lead to a loss of jobs for individuals drains one's emotional reserves. Fear, anxiety, guilt, feelings of failure, anger, and a desire to "run away" permeate one's thoughts. Without appropriate outlets to deal with these gripping feelings, the manager can become paralyzed by the emotional content and begin to make poor decisions about direction and strategy.

This negative spiral could lead to the ultimate demise of the department. If the director is perceived as ineffectual, there may be an increased likelihood to dismiss the leadership and consolidate the department under the leadership of another manager. This is not to suggest that consolidation occurs only in response to a leadership failure, but it is a significant factor when administration begins evaluating who is most qualified to assume increased administrative responsibilities.

Strategy 5: Manage Organizational Uncertainty

The final strategy focuses on managing organizational uncertainty. Organizational retrenchment is a process characterized by chronic uncertainty. Managers are taught rational decision-making models that emphasize a thorough analysis of relevant information and the selection of the alternatives based on an assessment of this information. This decision-making process is conducted within the domain of established organizational goals and missions that guide decisions and action (Hirschhorn, 1983). During times of retrenchment, managers may be called upon to make decisions at the same time that organizational goals and missions are being reevaluated. Decisions may need to be made for a future direction that has yet to be determined. Environmental information is also changing so that the data that inform decisions today may change radically within a short period of time. A major change in governmental regulation for reimbursement can throw financial projections into disarray. So how is a manager expected to plan for the future using data that may turn out to be irrelevant down the road?

Health care is changing at such a rapid rate that it has been described by many as chaotic. All the old ways of doing business no longer are able to help managers cope with such a changing environment. The result is that staff and managers are now experiencing the workplace as tumultuous and chaotic. People ask: "When are things going to get back to normal? When will we have some stability again?"

Managing during times of chronic uncertainty calls for a greatly expanded repertoire of skills that managers are only now beginning to develop. Our definitions of success have to change from maintaining a stable department to successfully managing constant change. In the past, a department undergoing constant change would have been evaluated by others as having a problem with leadership. Today, a manager's worth is directly related to the ability to manage constant change. Peters (1988) suggests that a manager who is not engaging daily in a change process is not effective.

Strategies for Managing Organizational Uncertainty

How can a manager be successful in an environment where the rules keep changing and even one's basic mission is constantly being called into question? How can one effectively manage uncertainty when the very nature of the environment fosters uncertainty? There are several useful strategies for managing under conditions of uncertainty (Hirschhorn, 1983):

- Create organizational structures that maximize program flexibility so that staff can respond to an array of opportunities and threats.
- Simultaneously examine future goals as well as historical strengths throughout the decision-making process.
- Encourage appropriate staff participation throughout the process.

Creating Programmatic Flexibility

Programmatic flexibility is a significant departure from historical staffing patterns that emphasized specialization. Traditionally, professional development followed a course that moved from generalist to specialist. With increased experience, social workers carved out an area of expertise that narrowed their practice in order to achieve greater depth in skills and knowledge. The move now is away from increased specialization toward generalist practice in order to increase flexibility within staffing patterns and service delivery. Managers must reexamine the skills mix and staffing patterns of their personnel in order to achieve greater flexibility. Managers need to be able to respond to rapid change, shifting resources to address peaks and valleys in need, new program initiatives, and reductions in services. This is extremely difficult when staff define their roles according to rigid boundaries of specializations. We need to move from being a "perinatal social worker" to a "pediatric social worker," from a "heart transplant social worker" to a "transplant social worker," from a "cardiology social worker" to an "internal medicine social worker." Three factors minimize commitment to fixed structures and procedures (Hirschhorn, 1983):

- Development of teams
- Development of organizational designs that emphasize task interdependence
- Development of a learning culture that encourages skill expansion

The use of teams is not new to the health care arena. Academicians and practitioners have been fascinated by their functioning, or lack of functioning, for over two decades. Teams continue to hold opportunity for developing cost-efficient models for service delivery if used effectively. A key to success in this health care environment is to maximize the skill repertoire of the members and then use the full complement of skills to accomplish the task. This requires that the members are committed to the team and equally share in the work, responsibility, and accountability.

An important component of team development, which is essential to ensuring flexibility, is interdependence of tasks among team members. One director of social work has been experimenting with a small work group design in which about three social work staff work together as a team. The team is responsible for service delivery to several services (e.g., cardiology, neurology, general medicine, rheumatology). Work is distributed within the team either through triage mechanisms or primary and secondary assignments. For example, one team member may be the primary worker for cardiology but each of the other members of the group provide backup for overload, vacation, sickness, or other types of leave. The staff on the floors become familiar with working with three social work staff members and begin to relate to the team rather than one social worker. The social workers cross-train so that they develop a repertoire of skills and knowledge that keeps them stimulated and growing professionally. The success of this approach has been the flexibility achieved with staffing. Team members can respond to shifting patterns in census, back each other up as members pursue temporary reassignments or engage in other types of professional activity, and provide an excellent forum in which to orient new staff.

To be successful in developing a flexible work force, management must commit to providing adequate resources for training. If the hospital is undergoing resizing, managers should advocate with the human resource or personnel department to set aside sufficient funds to retrain staff for new positions. Managers should also think carefully before giving up training and travel monies as part of their cost-efficiencies. It is easy to relinquish these nonpersonnel-related expenses, but this may represent another example of a short-term strategy that may have long-term negative consequences.

As organizations look to staff to do "more with less," take on added responsibilities, or change roles or functions, there must be sufficient resources to help them make these transitions and to reward their commitment to the organization. How can we expect staff to develop new skills if we give away all the money used for training? One of the most valued rewards by professional staff is the opportunity to grow professionally. How do we reward staff who go the extra mile, who give a little bit more to get the work done, if we eliminate training dollars? We need to invest in the future of our departments if we expect to face the future with qualified staff. That future may rest on our ability to provide support for training and skill development that will position us for the future.

Looking to the Future and the Past

New models of decision making may be necessary during times of organizational retrenchment. Traditional models emphasize the need for a clear understanding of organizational mission and a vision of future goals. This perspective set the context in which decisions were made. While an eye on the future will continue to be of importance, looking back at historical information may also be useful.

As managers face tough choices about where to reduce or eliminate services, it is helpful to stand back and look at one's historical roots within the organization. Managers need to ask: "What are the distinctive competencies that define and shape social work services? What has the organization valued over the years from the social work department?" It may be necessary to draw back to these core services as the department regroups for future growth.

Diane Anderson, associate hospital administrator for patient care services at the University of Washington Medical Center, described the resizing process as similar to pruning a bush. Not every branch gets cut when pruning. The gardener wants to prune the bush correctly so that it fosters new growth in the desired direction, but not so much that it kills the bush. Here lies the challenge for managers. In reducing services, it will be necessary to cut. One way of knowing just where or how far to cut would be to move back in the direction of the core services that have been the historical strength of the department. The manager should also take care to preserve the branches of the department that will provide growth in the desired direction. This could also include investing in new programs to encourage the desired growth.

The case example in chapter 3 regarding short-term versus long-term strategies illustrates this point. Recall that the departmental managers were faced with a 7 percent reduction and chose to reduce services in the psychiatry service. On the surface, one may question this decision given social work's historical roots in the mental health system. However, in this particular hospital, the psychiatry program was relatively weak and not a high priority for the hospital or medical school. It was not considered a "center of excellence" nor were there any future plans for the expansion of beds allocated to this program. The social work department did not draw strength from its involvement in this program, although it did through its involvement in the medical and surgical specialties. These latter services were slated for growth and three of the four "centers of excellence" for the hospital fell within these specialties. This is one reason why the managers chose to cut psychiatry rather than medical or surgical areas.

Having selected psychiatry as the target for cuts, the next decision was how to reduce staffing. Historically, staff with a master's degree in social work (MSW) provided comprehensive services to psychiatry patients, including psychosocial assessments, discharge planning, and family treatment. Over the years, the MSW staff migrated to a more narrowly defined role of providing family therapy. Psychosocial assessments were only performed for those families receiving family therapy from the MSW and discharge planning was relegated to the bachelor-prepared social worker (BSW). If one draws on the historical core, the social work role would include discharge planning and psychosocial assessments as well as family treatment. Legal mandates also supported a move in this direction because external reviewers from government payers required psychosocial assessments for all psychiatric patients as well as evidence of appropriate and effective discharge planning.

With fewer staff members to deliver services, the managers consciously redefined the role of the MSWs to return to this historical core. The role of social work on the psychiatry service was redefined as, in order of priority: (1) provide psychosocial assessment and discharge planning for every patient admitted to the psychiatric service, and (2) provide family treatment, specifically to facilitate complex discharges or eliminate barriers to the patient's ability to maximize acute care treatment. The managers of this department strongly believed that the expansion of social work services two years later was directly related to the redefinition of the social work role to this historical core.

As managers face the difficult task of restructuring and resizing social work services, they must walk a narrow line between investing in the future and supporting existing programs. Although returning to the historical core can provide some answers, it is not sufficient to position the department for the future. Managers must also commit time and resource to new programs and new approaches to service delivery. It is difficult to invest in new programs when money is tight and staff in existing programs are being displaced. It is this entrepreneurial spirit that must be nurtured in order to position for the future, particularly if the organizational culture promotes innovation. Not all organizations value entrepreneurial thinking and to engage in this type of activity could produce negative outcomes for the manager. Once again, a thorough evaluation of the environment is critical. It can also be risky because failure takes on greater meaning when resources are at such a premium. But, the literature suggests that the successful manager of the future will possess these entrepreneurial qualities (Gilmore and Peter, 1987; Brown and McCool, 1987; Kazemek and Grauman, 1989).

Encouraging Staff Participation

As discussed in chapter 3, there is ambivalence regarding the importance of staff participation in the resizing process. A positive aspect of staff involvement is that it tends to reduce anxiety by reducing some of the uncertainty. The more staff are informed and can make informed decisions regarding their future, the more they will be able to cope with the uncertainty of a chaotic work environment.

Hirschhorn (1983) suggests five strategies for reducing staff uncertainty. Many of these have already been discussed within other sections, but it is helpful to review these strategies again from the perspective of reducing uncertainty:

- Clarify the values of the agency and a sense of fundamental commitments.
- Clarify the agency: Who is responsible for what activities?
- Clarify the time line for decisions.
- Legitimize the work of worrying.
- Make robust decisions.

The literature in social work administration has emphasized the importance of values and ethical imperatives in managerial behavior (Reisch and Taylor, 1983). The values and norms that will guide the downsizing process need to be discussed early on so that workers can know what to expect. Such values as a worker's right to privacy, self-determination, and respect will set the tone for how staff are informed about decisions that will affect them, how much advance notice staff receive so that they have sufficient time to seek other employment, and the type of departmental support provided to assist workers to locate other positions. Staff anxiety will be reduced and their trust will grow if they feel the manager's decision-making process is guided by ethical standards (Johnson and Berger, 1990).

The second strategy, clarifying the agency, focuses on the delineation of roles regarding who will fulfill the various functions associated with downsizing. If the department has multiple staff at the management level, the ability to delegate the various roles is easier. If the department has only one manager, collaborative arrangements with other department administrators or with superiors may be advantageous.

A director of a small social work department, in which she was the only management staff, described working with her supervisor to delineate roles. The supervisor held several meetings with the staff and assumed primary responsibility for communicating organizational information to the staff as well as receiving their input. This allowed the director to more effectively manage the affective component of the process within the department. The hospital administrator communicated global decisions regarding how much needed to be cut while the director dealt directly with those affected. In this way, the administrator absorbed much of the anger, freeing the director to manage the adjustment of staff to the changes.

A note of caution with this model is to ensure that the director does not appear to have no control or influence over decision making. If the director comes across as passive, the staff could feel that they are leaderless. It is important that the director and administrator be perceived as working together.

Another example comes from a large, complex social work department with multiple levels of staff. When the need to resize was mandated by hospital administration, the director and associate director of a social work department delineated various roles that needed to be fulfilled and assigned responsibility among themselves and the three supervisors (Johnson and Berger, 1990). First, the process of resizing required constant surveillance in both the department and the medical center (e.g., internal and external communities to the department, according to the political-economic framework). Supervisors assumed responsibility for monitoring their respective areas, coordinating their efforts through weekly management team meetings with the director and associate director. The director focused attention on the wider hospital community.

Two-way communication was critical: to ensure a consistent message from hospital administration to the staff and clear communication of the department's position to hospital administration. The associate director monitored the pulse of the department, relaying information from the director to staff and vice versa.

Another important role involved how decisions were made and how staff were informed about major decisions. Although the management team of this department valued staff participation, it felt that the director should assume ultimate decision-making authority. The director was responsible for informing any staff who were affected by downsizing decisions. The associate director and the supervisors were then available to help staff deal with the emotional content. Staff anger was more likely to be directed at the messenger, the director, thus freeing the other managers to help with their emotional reactions.

There are other ways to handle these roles as well. Some departments report that their supervisors assume responsibility for informing those affected. Others indicate that hospital administration or personnel participate in this process. There is no one way to handle these roles. Directors must determine which works best for their own departments, given the unique characteristics of each setting and management style.

Clarifying the time line for decisions, the third strategy, may be one of the most important strategies for reducing anxiety. The "not knowing" can intensify the feelings of helplessness and worry with no end in sight. Realistic benchmarks for the process need to be established and communicated to staff. Equally important, management needs to stick to this time line or communicate extensions as soon as possible. If changes in the time line occur too often it can have the same effect as if there were no time line. This is why it is important that the benchmarks are realizable.

The fourth strategy, legitimizing worry, is described in the beginning of this chapter, so discussion will move to the final strategy, making robust decisions. Robust decisions are those that can be adapted to changing environments without major reworking. In essence, they can stand up to change.

A common complaint by those involved in resizing is that their environment feels so unstable and chaotic. Many of the factors contributing to this atmosphere are outside the control of managers (e.g., the need to resize, personnel policies that require specific steps, etc.). However, managers can add to this craziness if their decisions are so narrowly focused that changes in the environment require a new set of decisions that require major changes on the part of staff. Feelings of uncertainty escalate, producing heightened anxiety.

An example of a robust decision is to move to service teams rather than individual service assignments (as described in chapter 4 in relation to flexible staffing patterns). If service priorities or the number of beds allocated to specific services change, the team can adjust more easily than can individuals. If staffing within the social work team needs to be reduced further, the team is already familiar with all the services and can move more quickly into alternative models for service delivery.

Another example of a robust decision has to do with administrative restructuring. A director of a large department of social work implemented reductions in the management structure of the department as part of an organizational cost-efficiency mandate. Originally, the department had four levels of manageent from the line supervisors to the director (see figure 2, next page).

The proposal was to eliminate two of the levels, leaving only the director and assistant director levels. This proposal would have been effective as long as the director was only responsible for the social work department. However, the organization was undergoing major departmental consolidations and the director of social work was being considered for absorbing several other departments. This decision was not to be made for at least 6 to 12 months. The director recognized that this restructuring would be very difficult and disruptive to the department and did not want to reorganize again should her administrative responsibilities expand. The director moved to a more robust decision by creating the following structure (see figure 3, page 56).

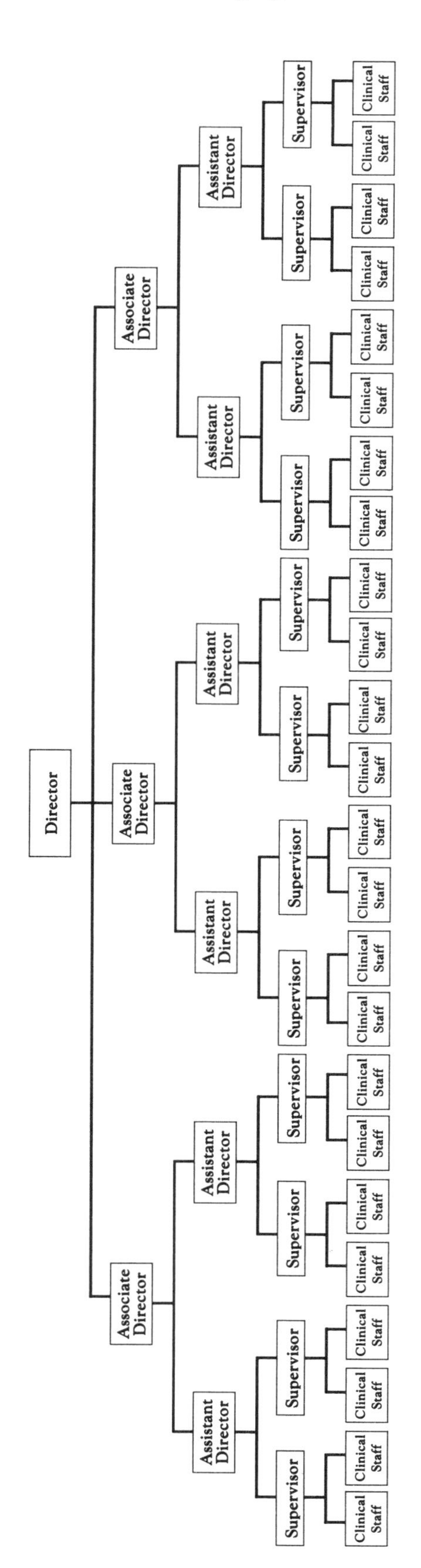

Figure 2. Pre-Resizing Departmental Management Structure

Figure 3: Post-Resizing Departmental Structure

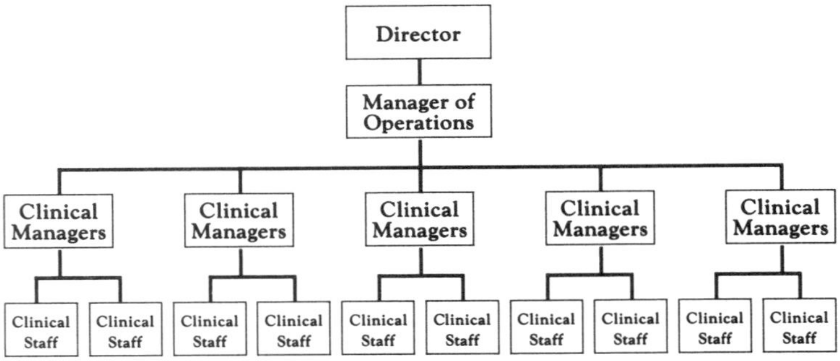

Director

Manager of Operations

Clinical Managers | Clinical Managers | Clinical Managers | Clinical Managers | Clinical Managers

Clinical Staff | Clinical Staff | Clinical Staff | Clinical Staff | Clinical Staff | Clinical Staff | Clinical Staff | Clinical Staff | Clinical Staff | Clinical Staff

This structure utilized the same number of staff but created a "manager of operations" position. If other departments were then consolidated, a manager position could be appointed for the new areas, and the administrative structure could remain intact.

Employees will continue to yearn for the "stable" environments of the past, but these are never likely to return. The only constant in the present environment is change, and managers need to adapt their decision-making styles to respond to a continuously shifting and changing world.

Conclusion

When the reality of downsizing or resizing hits, managers will become immersed in the technical aspects of the process. How to make the cuts? How to reorganize? How to develop new revenue streams? It is important to remember that health care is predominantly a service organization in which people are the largest component of the production cycle. If staff's ability to cope is seriously damaged by their emotional turmoil, then the efficiency and effectiveness of the organization will be seriously damaged. Resizing usually occurs in response to a poor financial picture and any further damage to the organization's financial viability is an important concern.

The emotional context of resizing is as important as the technical component. It cannot be avoided or ignored. If managed effectively, it can produce a more conducive environment for change. If handled badly, it could lead to the eventual demise of the social work department.

Chapter 5

Managing the Layoff Process: Planning for Those Who Leave and Those Who Stay

One of the most difficult tasks of an administrator is to lay off personnel. A manager may have the experience of "letting people go," but this is usually related to disciplinary action. Although the manager may regret the action, he or she feels justified in dismissing the individual. The responsibility for the dismissal falls on the employee who did not perform according to clearly articulated expectations.

Layoffs associated with resizing strategies don't carry this same emotional protective shield. Those affected are in no way responsible for the outcome. Responsibility cannot be assigned to the worker, leaving the manager and administration to carrying the burden of guilt. Even if the manager agrees with the organizational mandate to reduce cost, it is little solace for the emotional turmoil of laying off personnel.

A layoff is defined as "an action taken by an organization to reduce employment or labor costs . . . an employee is placed on leave that can be temporary, indefinite, or permanent" (Vestal, 1986, p. 196). It is not an action to take lightly because the legal ramifications can be dramatic. A manager should proceed through this process very carefully with close consultation from the personnel department.

There are three key stages to the layoff process. Managers must pay careful attention to each of the following stages in order to achieve an effective process that will have the least deleterious effect on staff morale and productivity:

- Making the layoff decision
- Establishing the plan for layoffs
- Taking care of the survivors

Making the Layoff Decision

Deciding who should be laid off will create a struggle for the managers as they balance issues of equity and efficiency. There may be an initial leaning on the part of social work managers toward equity because of their professional value system. Managers should think carefully as they weigh these two variables because the choice will have long-term consequences for the viability of the department. In some organizations, this decision will be defined by personnel policies, leaving the manager no choice.

If equity is the guiding principle for the layoff process, managers will use impersonal criteria for making their decisions. A seniority system is one of the most common strategies called upon to achieve equity. These systems call for layoffs according to the policy of "last hired, first fired."

Even with something as clear-cut as seniority, the process can get confusing. It is important that the manager clearly understand the organization's position regarding issues of seniority. Seniority may be defined within job classification (clinical social worker, associate director, social work supervisor) rather than by department. In this situation, the last hired within a specific classification would be laid off as opposed to the last hired across the entire department.

The manager must also determine whether the organization has a "bumping" policy. Bumping means that an individual who is laid off has the right to take a position within a lower job classification if there is an individual in that classification with less seniority. In essence, the individual who is laid off can claim the position of the less senior worker and literally have him or her removed.

For example, a social work supervisor with five years of seniority who is laid off is eligible to take the position of a clinical social worker who has four years of experience. Now, it is the clinical social worker who is laid off. However, that social worker can now claim the position of a social worker with three years of experience and so on. This "musical chairs" approach to the process can be extremely disruptive to the work group and devastating to morale. If "bumping" rights do exist, the manager would be advised to begin the layoff process at the lowest level and then reclassify staff into lower-level positions as needed, unless the manager can make a case for why the most senior worker could not perform the duties of the less senior worker.

Issues of job performance are the only criteria that negate the impact of seniority systems. A clear and compelling argument must be made that includes the following elements:

- The senior worker could not perform the duties.
- The senior worker could not be trained within a reasonable period of time to perform the duties.
- The absence of these duties will have a significant negative impact on service delivery and/or organizational functioning.

Proving this inability is not an easy task. The manager must compile data that demonstrate the lack of knowledge and skill as well as substantiate why the worker could not learn the skill in a sufficient period of time. First, what is a sufficient period of time? Is it three months or six months? How do you know they could not learn the skill? Who will pay for the retraining? Managers would be advised to work very closely with their personnel representatives if attempting to dismiss seniority using this method.

The problem with a seniority system is that it commits what Levine (1978) calls the "paradox of irreducible wholes." It assumes that the organization can dismantle in the same order it assembled. However, organizational and program development don't occur according to such an orderly process. Layoff by seniority can often devastate new programs that may hold the greatest opportunity for organizational recovery. Even the time period to retrain more senior staff could significantly hurt the program, to say nothing of the disruption to delicate interpersonal relationships among team members that are often the key to team functioning.

Another fallacy of seniority systems is that they often are not equitable. Minority groups are often most affected by such systems since they are frequently the newest members of the group. It is not uncommon to find that minorities are more likely to experience layoffs during periods of organizational downsizing.

The alternative approach is to base the layoff decision according to issues of efficiency. From this perspective, the manager must determine which staff and/or programs are most capable of maintaining departmental function while moving the department into the future. Managers will need to draw upon data that speak to organizational priorities, levels of productivity within both the organization and the department, skill mix of departmental members, and any other useful information in this decision-making process. In essence, this type of decision making is what is captured in chapter 1's analogy of the boat taking a "hit." The manager must determine which staff are most capable of keeping the department afloat so that it can steer into the future.

The problem with using efficiency as the guide is that it can lead to litigation. The legal risks associated with layoffs occur when established policies and procedures are violated and/or employees to be laid off are subjected to partiality, discrimination, and arbitrariness (Vestal, 1986). The layoff process is not to be used to weed out poor performers or problem staff. That is what the disciplinary process is for. While efficiency may be the more responsible managerial approach, an entrenched personnel system and organizational policies often make this an impossible alternative.

Establishing the Layoff Plan

Once the decision of who will face layoffs has been determined, the manager needs to establish a plan for implementation. This plan should address how to communicate layoff decisions, develop timeliness for the process, prepare managers to conduct layoff interviews, and develop employee exit procedures (Vestal, 1986). This plan must also include who will be responsible for informing staff.

This decision must be part of a broader plan for the delineation of roles in the resizing process (see chapter 3). The manager must keep in mind that the messenger is likely to be the recipient of employee anger, and therefore, may be less capable of helping the employees deal with the emotional impact. That is why the manager should carefully think through this decision. It is important that the employee have an individual within the organization who can help them address the emotional impact of this news, particularly if that function cannot be handled within the department. Even if departmental support is available, it may be better to utilize a program outside the department (e.g., an outplacement service).

Conducting a layoff interview can be extremely challenging and difficult. Even if employees have anticipated that their positions are in jeopardy, the emotional reaction to the news can be devastating. Because the layoff process is legally risky, it is essential that those individuals who are conducting layoff interviews be adequately trained. Training topics might include organizational policies and procedures related to layoffs and benefits for individuals who are laid off, how to compose a layoff letter, how to inform employees that their positions have been eliminated, and how to access career transition programs, including outplacement services and employee assistance programs. Most, if not all, of these issues are likely to surface in the layoff interview. Managers must also learn how to deal with their own reactions and where they can find help.

If a formalized training program is not available, personnel departments may be an alternative resource. Personnel representatives are often prepared to meet with managers to provide consultation regarding the process. Sample letters for layoffs may be available as well as brochures and checklists to provide correct information and knowledge about procedures. Employee representatives may also be available to meet directly with employees to ensure that they understand the layoff processes and procedures as well as their rights, and to help employees sort through their feelings.

Many organizations set up formalized programs that help employees address the multitude of issues that a layoff will create. Outplacement and career transition programs are assuming greater visibility in health care organizations as resizing becomes a common occurrence. These programs often provide services not only to the employee but also to their families because both will be affected by job loss.

Before the layoff interview is conducted, the manager should have a set plan for the exit process. Will employees be escorted to their offices to collect their belongings and then to the door? After the layoff interview, will the employees be allowed to leave for the day? If there is advance notification, what allowances will be made for the employee to seek other employment or participate in career transition services? The following example illustrates one type of exit process instituted in a hospital. It was a very formal and structured process that was adhered to by every manager:

- All managers were required to participate in a day-long training session regarding the layoff process before conducting a layoff interview.
- The layoff interview was conducted as early as possible in the working day.
- Immediately following the interview, the employee met his or her personnel representative in a prearranged appointment and then received release time for the remainder of the day.
- For the next four days, the employee participated in a precheduled career transition program offered by the hospital.

The hospital also built in additional incentives to facilitate the employees' job search. All employees were given at least 30 days notice (employees with over ten years of seniority were given 90 days notice) during which they would receive pay but were not required to report to work. This was not construed as severance pay. It was viewed as paid work time to try to locate another job. Employees who returned to work (e.g., before their 30- or 90-day cutoff) would be eligible to interview, on work time, for other positions both internal and external to the organization. All hospital materials (e.g., keys, pagers, identification badges, etc.) were turned into the office manager prior to the worker's departure. Although not required by hospital procedure, the director of social work conducted an exit interview on the employee's last day of reporting to work.

It is critical that managers develop and implement a finely tuned and well-orchestrated layoff process. It can reduce potential errors leading to litigation. It can also decrease the emotional roller coaster that can be experienced by the employee, manager, and other staff. But this process is insufficient if it does not also include a plan for addressing the concerns and issues of the remaining staff. An important first step is to develop a process that treats individuals who are leaving with dignity and respect. This goes a long way toward gaining the support and trust of staff who will stay. Developing complete and effective strategies for caring for the survivors must then occur to ensure a smoother transition to the new structure of the organization.

Caring for the Survivors

One of the most neglected steps in the resizing process is addressing the needs of the employees who will remain to do the work. Much of the manager's time and energy has been drained upon completion of the layoff process; there is little left to give to the staff who remain. There may even be a sense of anger toward staff who are seeking assurance or support from leadership or complaining about their jobs. It is not uncommon to hear comments like: "What are they complaining about? At least they have their jobs!" According to Weinstein and Leibman (1991, p. 33), "The future of the organization will depend upon those who stay—and whether they can embrace the new vision, recommit to new goals, and focus on their newly defined jobs."

Downsizing often damages a worker's sense of trust in the organization and leadership. It disrupts a fundamental relationship between the organization and the individual that is characterized by secure, long-term employment in exchange for acceptable work performance (Smallwood and Jacobsen, 1987). Employees' feelings of security are destroyed and they worry, "Am I next in line to be let go?" This diminished trust can manifest itself behaviorally and has been described in the literature as the "survivor's syndrome" (Smallwood and Jacobsen, 1987).

The "survivor's syndrome" is a set of common behaviors displayed by staff who remain after a layoff process. It can appear as anger, paranoia, defensiveness, anxiety, and fear. Increased dissatisfaction with the manager, constant complaints about the work being unmanageable, and low morale are likely to occur. There is a tendency for staff to retreat to safe positions, even as innovation and creativity are needed to rebuild or create programs, or to become highly political. Smallwood and Jacobson (1987) have described two unproductive types of employee behavior that may emerge: the "vanishing employee" and the "politician."

Vanishing employees cope with the insecurity created by the lack of trust by keeping a low profile. They tend to avoid risks and resist change that will bring attention to their work. Their philosophy becomes: "If they can't see me, they can't fire me" (Smallwood and Jacobson, 1987, p. 44).

The philosophy of the politicians is that the only thing that counts to the organization is the financial "bottom line." Rather than discussing how the organization should address important changes or concerns, they continuously reframe issues in terms of the bottom line. Although the bottom line is of critical importance during a fiscal crisis, it is not the only important issue. Rebuilding trust and morale and searching for creative and innovative solutions to problems created by the changes are equally important. An overemphasis on the political realm can inhibit the creative energy that is so necessary to the rebuilding process.

Another common reaction among staff is "survivor's guilt" (Smallwood and Jacobson, 1987; Weinstein and Leibman, 1991). Employees struggle with their own grief over multiple loss: loss of friends, colleagues, and familiar work processes. They feel a sense of guilt for having survived the layoffs while their friends lost their jobs. This survivor's guilt can be exacerbated if the survivors do not understand how the decisions are made regarding who is laid off. It is critical that management discuss how decisions are made and who made them. Even if this was discussed before layoffs started, it is worth repeating during and after the layoff process is completed.

A common mistake of managers is to present the resizing and restructuring as an event rather than an ongoing process of change in response to a constantly shifting environment. Managers imply or sometimes directly state that once the layoffs are complete, there will be no more layoffs. That may be true today but what about one, two, or five years from now?

It is understandable why managers are quick to make these promises. They are often communicating their own hopes and fantasies. To entertain the thought of further reductions is too distressful, so they believe that these cuts will be a onetime event.

Another explanation has to do with the belief that staff morale will improve once the cuts are over, and that such promises will rebuild a sense of security. They can actually have the opposite effect. If further reductions are required, even five years down the road, some staff will remember the promises. This "broken promise" can destroy trust and make it extremely difficult to rebuild the department with the remaining staff.

It is critical that management turn to rebuilding trust and service delivery systems once the layoff process has been completed. Senior management must "explain to those who remain what is happening, why it is happening, and what it all means" (Weinstein and Leibman, 1991, p. 34). Staff need to understand the new direction and vision of the organization so they can become invested in the new goals and objectives. Work process redesign is essential to prevent workers from feeling overburdened. It is amazing that, in spite of major reductions in resources, people will behave as if the work itself won't change. If it doesn't change, burnout is imminent.

Weinstein and Leibman (1991) describe the following strategies for the survivors:

- Provide an atmosphere in which survivors deal with their sense of loss.
- Rechannel energy.
- Reward top performance.
- Provide employees with the tools to deal with the future.
- Encourage open communication.

It is surprising how much benefit is derived by allowing staff to deal with the multitude of losses that resizing creates. As described earlier, many managers want to put everything behind them once the layoffs are complete; the thought of spending time talking about it seems unbearable. Yet, this time is critical to moving forward. Survivors need to put their conflicting feelings and concerns into some perspective. This is a time for management to listen to staff's questions about what has happened, where they are going, and what is in store for them in terms of duties and responsibilities. Although emotionally wrenching, it is a fundamental step in rebuilding trust and morale (Weinstein and Leibman, 1991).

The second strategy is to rechannel all this emotion into positive action. Rather than enable staff to become "vanishing" or "political" employees, managers need to redirect employees' energies into activities that encourage their participation in the development of innovative and creative approaches to dealing with the changes that have occurred. One department of social work created a variety of task-focused groups to deal with several issues, including departmental restructuring, discharge planning, and fee-for-service. Each group was given an opportunity to develop goals and objectives and to recommend strategies for achieving them. Staff channeled all their energy into these task groups, which enabled them to feel empowered and creative, while contributing to positive change for the department. One of the outstanding suggestions was to develop self-managed work groups that enabled the department to eliminate one level in the administrative hierarchy.

The third strategy, and one of the greatest challenges of management, is to create an incentive system when there are limited resources. As organizations flatten their structures, promotional opportunities dwindle, cutbacks lead to fewer and smaller salary programs, and training budgets are significantly reduced or eliminated. Managers have fewer incentives with which to reward outstanding performers. These departments become subject to what has been described in academia as a "brain drain." The "stars" are able to locate other opportunities outside the organization, leaving the department with staff who may be least prepared to carry it into the future.

Managers must be innovative in their approaches to rewarding outstanding performance. Utilizing "merit" systems is one approach. Social workers have shied away from these types of salary programs because of value conflicts. However, across-the-board raises have often been questioned because of their tendency to promote mediocrity. Instituting "merit" salary programs may be the only financial incentive available.

It is also important to remember that professionals are more likely to be motivated by opportunity for professional growth than by money. This is an important reason to protect training dollars rather than sacrificing them early on. Managers must work directly with employees to explore what their professional goals are and to try to create opportunities to achieve them. Although promotion may not be possible, professional growth may be achieved through the assignment of special projects, new service assignments, program development, and student programs. Each manager must explore all possible incentives in order to hold employee commitment to the organization.

The fourth strategy, dealing with the future, is an ongoing process and has been discussed at several points in this book. Employees need to have a realistic picture of what is ahead. They need to understand that the only constant is change and that new paradigms for practice are essential. The dream of returning to a stable environment needs to be replaced. Learning how to effectively cope with change will more effectively prepare staff to meet an ever shifting and shaking future.

The survivors must also have the skills to carry the organization into the future. If there are fewer people to do the work, these individuals must be highly skilled and motivated to do a better job. Resources must be available to retrain or enhance skills.

Finally, for resizing to be effective, employees need accurate and timely communication. Once again, the importance of effective communication has been stressed throughout this book. Information is one of the most powerful resources within any organization. Giving people information is giving them the power to make informed decisions, as well as creating an environment in which each individual feels respected. The ultimate success of the organization may rest on management's ability to maintain effective communication with the remaining employees.

For the past decade, resizing has been a necessity for most organizations. Although it is important that managers develop skills in determining how and where to make reductions, it is equally important that they acquire skills to effectively implement these changes so that the organization continues as a viable institution. The success of any resizing program may rest on the ability of managers to successfully handle the layoff process. This entails both the emotional and technical aspects, as well as an organized program to manage those staff who remain. Henkoff (1990, p. 40) describes an interesting caricature of a manager engaged in resizing: "a harried, still in shock . . . executive who returns from the office and exclaims to his wife: 'Honey, I shrunk the company! What do I do now?' " Managers must be prepared to answer this question if resizing and restructuring programs are to succeed.

Chapter 6

Facing the Future Prepared

The health care arena can be described as changing at a more rapid rate than ever before. Much of this change is in response to a shrinking resource pool as "cost containment" becomes the guiding principle for decision making. Given today's competitive pressures, health care organizations need to create climates that encourage rapid change and entrepreneurial behavior (Gilmore and Peter, 1987) while at the same time holding down costs. Social work administrators need to prepare themselves to manage effectively in this constantly changing environment.

New Measures of Success

An essential aspect of this change is the need to modify measures of success. Managers tend to measure success according to growth criteria. It is not uncommon to hear managers sharing the size of their department, their social worker-to-bed ratio, and the amount and quality of departmental space as banners of success. In today's health care environment, increased numbers are becoming more problematic. As resources continue to shrink, adding staff as the primary strategy to achieve goals and objectives can set up a model doomed to failure.

What is needed are new definitions of success in terms of positive change as well as increases. Managers need to recognize opportunities that exist within current resource allocations. The manager may have enough resources, just not the right *kind* or appropriately dispersed. Success may lie in expanding services within existing resources through restructuring and resizing strategies.

Resizing and Restructuring Are Not a Fad

Organizational resizing is not a fad. It is in response to a changing fiscal picture for health care that is likely to continue for some time in the future. Managers need to be prepared to embrace these changes rather than avoid them.

This book has outlined various steps and issues that need to be addressed as managers engage in resizing strategies. It begins by evaluating the organization, both internally and externally. A political-economic framework offers one model for this evaluation process. It is in this initial assessment phase that the manager uncovers discrepancies between the actual and the desired state of affairs and develops some notions of what can be done to diminish the differences (Brager and Holloway, 1978). Relevant data are collected and organized, using a variety of methods including many that already exist within the organization.

This information must be used to shape the decision-making process regarding resizing strategies. Several issues related to resizing were examined in chapter 3. There are no easy answers or "cookbook" approaches to designing one's program. Resizing must be based on a careful examination of organizational factors and issues that shape the most effective strategies within one's own organization.

The Elements of Success

Kazemek and Channon (1988) encourage managers to adopt a "targeted" versus "untargeted" approach to the resizing process. The "untargeted" approach is characterized by short-term strategies such as across-the-board cuts, voluntary excused absences, and attrition or early retirement. Although often easier to implement, their long-term consequences can be disastrous. A "targeted" approach is recommended, which is characterized by strategic decision making based on careful analysis of the organization, management structure, and productivity. Resizing decisions are based on this current information and target specific programs or employees.

Throughout this process, communication is critical. Managers are advised to communicate frequently and openly with employees to reduce uncertainty and anxiety. These are two of the most critical barriers to effective change and need to be managed carefully. The "human component" should not be lost in all the technical processes. Change occurs *with* people, not around them. The human elements must be attended to, particularly the emotional context of the resizing process.

This human component is especially relevant when implementing reductions in staff. The layoff process needs to receive much attention, ensuring that people are treated with dignity and respect. Careful attention must also be given to the "survivors."

The success of the organization will depend on the ability of the remaining staff to commit to the new goals and objectives and perform the work with a commitment to quality. This human component may be pivotal to ensuring an effective transition.

Although resizing is often experienced as a new and often unpleasant challenge for social work administrators, it is important to recognize that it is a change strategy. Social workers are trained to be effective change agents and managers need to draw upon these skills to effectively implement resizing strategies. Schermerhorn (1981) has identified the following change inputs that are important as elements in any planned change strategy:

- *Planning.* Identifying the factors causing a need for change, gathering relevant data, selecting the change option from various alternatives, implementation and evaluation.
- *Direction.* Setting change goals, providing information on expected change benefits and consequences, developing a range of strategies and tactics to implement the change.
- *Power.* The use of personal and structural sources of power during the change effort to achieve identified goals and objectives.
- *Participation.* The presence of good communication between the manager and persons affected by a change.
- *Managerial support.* Seeking and providing support through the provision of resources necessary to help people incorporate the change.

These change inputs have been addressed throughout the book and often are found at the heart of any successful resizing strategy. The success of resizing strategies will ultimately rest with effective leadership.

The Search for Leadership

Organizational decline is a time when one's leadership skill and potential are seriously tested. Strong social work leadership is needed to face a health care environment that is constantly changing and often chaotic. Brown and McCool (1987) identify the following traits that will characterize the leader of the future:

- Healthy, energy-giving, and hard-working
- Creative, intuitive, and innovative
- Mission-oriented, entrepreneurial, and visionary

The health care environment is constantly bombarding the manager with change. Rather than responding with inertia and psychological shutdown from cognitive overload, managers must present themselves as being in charge and on top of things (Brown and McCool, 1987). This is not to be confused with false activism or optimism. What is needed is a realistic stance that conveys a "can-do" attitude about those things that can be changed.

Social work administrators need to keep their energy high and their senses sharp to respond to a rapidly changing organization. Successful leaders must recognize that the practice environment is ambiguous, confusing, dynamic, and complex (Biscoe, 1989). Managers must learn how to deal with stress and the emotional turmoil of resizing, particularly when it involves a reduction in staffing.

Creativity, intuition, and innovation are equally important. The most effective leaders must be open to new ideas and new ways of doing things. This sentiment is best captured by an anonymous quote (Biscoe, 1989, p. 114):

> If you always do what you have always done, you will always get what you have always got. What was always done hasn't seemed to work; therefore, "do something else" is the order of the day.

This is the time to stretch one's thinking. Engage in scenario-building exercises; ask "what if" questions about everything. Nothing is sacred when resizing calls for creative thinking and risk-taking.

Under the present financial pressures, managers must not only think about how to reduce but also about where to move forward. Probably one of the most difficult challenges is to support new programs and ventures while old ones are being eliminated or downsized, but this is why strong leadership is so essential during these times.

Entrepreneurial leadership requires individuals who thrive on uncertainty, change, and risk (Kazemek and Grauman, 1989). The social work administrator needs to lead, to set the course for the department to carry it into the future. It is this sense of the future that should shape the resizing decisions of today.

There is not an easy or neat answer to organizational resizing. It is a process of change in response to a chaotic health care environment that is declining financially. Resizing represents a new set of skills and issues that many social work administrators have not developed. This book is a beginning step in learning how to be an effective manager during organizational retrenchment.

The following quote by Kanter (1986, p. 21) sums up the type of change agent that is needed to implement effective resizing strategies:

> Change will always be a threat if it's done *to* people, if it's imposed and forced. "They're making me do it," the employees will cry. But change is an opportunity if it's accomplished by people. Then it is an opportunity to become heroes, to be involved in something larger than themselves. Few things can be more liberating for management and more encouraging of change and innovation.

Bibliography

Austin, M. J. Managing cutbacks in the 1980s. *Social Work*. 1984. 29(5):428-434.

Behn, R. D. Closing a government facility. *Public Administration Review*. 1978. 38(4):332-338.

Behn, R. D. How to terminate a public policy: A dozen hints for the would-be terminator. In: C. H. Levine, editor. *Managing Fiscal Stress: The Crisis in the Public Sector*. Chatham, NJ: Chatham House, 1978, pp. 327-342.

Behn, R. D. A symposium: Leadership in an era of retrenchment. *Public Administration Review*. 1980. 40(6):603-604.

Behn, R. D. Leadership for cut-back management: The use of corporate strategy. *Public Administration Review*. 1980. 40(6):613-620.

Berger, C. S. A political-economic analysis of hospital receptivity to social work. Ph.D. Dissertation, University of Southern California, Los Angeles, CA, 1982.

Berger, C. S. Downsizing by any other name means cutbacks. *Social Work Administration*. 1991. 17(2):8-10.

Berger, C. S. Enhancing social work influence in the hospital: Identifying sources of power. *Social Work in Health Care*. 1990. 15(2):77-93.

Biller, R. P. Leadership tactics for retrenchment. *Public Administration Review*. 1980. 40(6):604-609.

Biscoe, G. The changing scene in health care management. *International Nursing Review*. 1989. 36(4):113-116.

Brager, G., and Holloway, S. *Changing Human Service Organizations*. New York City: The Free Press, 1978.

Brewer, G. D. Termination: Hard choices—harder questions. *Public Administration Review*. 1978. 38(4):338-343.

Bridges, W. *Surviving Corporate Transitions*. New York City: Doubleday, 1988.

Brown, M., and McCool, B. P. High-performing managers: Leadership attributes for the 1990s. *Health Care Management Review*. 1987. 12(2):69-75.

Bruce, A., and Patterson, D. Resizing hospital nursing organizations, an alternative to downsizing. *Nursing Management*. 1987. 18(11):33-35.

Cameron, K. S. Managing turbulence, downsizing, and decline. *Dividend*. Fall 1990. pp. 4-7.

Cyert, R. M. The management of universities of constant or decreasing size. *Public Administration Review*. 1978. 38(4):344-349.

Dear, R. B., and Patti, R. J. Legislative advocacy: Seven effective tactics. *Social Work*. 1981. 26(4):289-296.

Downsizing: A matter of management philosophy. *Personnel Administrator*. 1988. 33(1):36-38.

Gilmore, T. N., and Peter, M. A. Managing complexity in health care settings. *Journal of Nursing Administration*. 1987. 17(1):11-17.

Glassberg, A. Reduction in force: Cost-effectiveness of alternative strategies. *Managing Fiscal Stress: The Crisis in the Public Sector*. Chatham, NJ: Chatham House, 1978, pp. 325-332.

Greenhalgh, L., and McKresie, R. B. Cost-effectiveness of alternative strategies for cut-back management. *Public Administration Review*. 1980. 40(6):575-584.

Henkoff, R. Cost cutting: How to do it right. *Fortune*. 1990. 121(8):40-49.

Hirschhorn, L. Firing good people. *Public Welfare*. 1982. 40(3):9-15.

Hirschhorn, L., editor. *Cutting Back: Retrenchment and Redevelopment in Human and Community Services*. San Francisco: Jossey-Bass, 1983.

Inglehart, A. P. Discharge planning: Professional perspectives versus organizational effects. *Social Work*. 1990. 15(4):301-309.

Johnson, R. S., and Berger, C. S. The challenge of change: Enhancing social work services at a time of cutback. *Health and Social Work*. 1990. 15(3):181-190.

Kanter, R. M. Becoming a healthcare change master. *Healthcare Executive*. 1986. 1(6):18-21.

Kazemek, E. A., and Channon, B. Avoiding the trauma of organizational downsizing. *Healthcare Financial Management*. 1988. 42(5):40-45, 48.

Kazemek E. A., and Grauman, D. M. Successful healthcare executives are entrepreneurs. *Healthcare Financial Management*. 1989. 43(2):82.

Levine, C. H. Organizational decline and cutback management. *Public Administration Review*. 1978. 38(4):316-325.

Levine, C. H. More on cutback management: Hard questions for hard times. *Public Administration Review*. 1979. 39(2):179-183.

Levine, C. H., editor. The new crisis in the public sector. *Managing Fiscal Stress: The Crisis in the Public Sector*. Chatham, NJ: Chatham House, 1978, pp. 327-342.

Levine, C. H., editor. *Managing Fiscal Stress: The Crisis in the Public Sector*. Chatham, NJ: Chatham House, 1978.

Lewis, C. W., and Logalbo, A. T. Cutback principles and practices: A checklist for managers. *Public Administration Review*. 1980. 40:184-188.

Longest, B. B., Jr. An external dependence perspective of organizational strategy and structure: The community hospital care. *Hospital and Health Services Administration*. 1981. 26:50-69.

Maricich, S. Downsizing. *Hospital Forum*. 1985. 28(4):19-23.

McTighe, J. J. Management strategies to deal with shrinking resources. *Public Administration Review*. 1979. 39(1):86-90.

Mitnick, B. M. Deregulation as a process of organizational reduction. *Public Administration Review*. 1978. 38(4):350-357.

Overman, S. The layoff legacy. *Human Resource Magazine*. 1991. 36:29-32.

Pawlak, E. J., Feter, S. C., and Fink, R. L. The politics of cutback management. *Administration in Social Work*. 1983. 7(2):1-10.

Peters, T. *Thriving on Chaos*. New York City: Alfred A. Knopf, 1988.

Potthoff, E. H, Jr. Pre-planning for budget reductions. *Public Management*. 1974. 57(3):13-14.

Reisch, M., and Taylor, C. L. Ethical guidelines for cutback management: A preliminary approach. *Administration in Social Work*. 1983. 7(3/4):59-72.

Rubin, I. Preventing or eliminating planned deficits: Restructuring political incentives. *Public Administration Review*. 1980. 40(6):621-626.

Schermerhorn, J. R., Jr. Guidelines for change in health care organizations. *Health Care Management Review*. 1981. 6(3):9-16.

Schmidt, W. H., and Tannenbaum, R. Management of differences. *Harvard Business Review*. 1960. 38(6):107-115.

Shaffer, M. J., and Shaffer, M. D. Clinical engineering in a downsizing environment. *Medical Instrumentation*. 1988. 22(4):201-204.

Shefter, M. New York City's fiscal crisis: The politics of inflation and retrenchment. *The Public Interest*. 1977. 48:98-127.

Sizing up downsizing. *Training*. 1990. 27(2):67.

Smallwood, W. N., and Jacobsen, E. Is there life after downsizing? *Personnel*. 1987. 64:42-46.

Starkweather, D. B., and Cook, K. S. Organization-environment relations. In: S. M. Shortess and A. D. Kulzany, editors. *Health Care Management: A Test in Organization Theory and Behavior Care Management*. New York City: John Wiley & Sons, 1988, pp. 344-378.

Staw, B. M., and Szwajkowski, E. The scarcity-munificence component of organizational environments and the commission of illegal acts. *Administrative Science Quarterly*. 1975. 20(3):345-354.

Stenberg, C. W. Beyond the days of wine and roses: Intergovernmental management in a cutback environment. *Public Administration Review*. 1981. 41(1):10-20.

Stewart, R. P. Watershed days: How will social work respond to the conservative revolution? *Social Work*. 1981. 26(4):271-273.

Terrell, P. Adapting to austerity: Human services after Proposition 13. *Social Work*. 1981. 26(4):275-281.

Turem, J. S., and Born, C. E. Doing more with less. *Social Work*. 1983. 28(3):206-210.

Van Sumeren, M. A. Organizational downsizing: Streamlining the health care organization. *Healthcare Financial Management*. 1986. 40(1):35-39.

Vestal, K. W. The manager's role in downsizing pediatric services. *Journal of Pediatric Nursing*. 1986. 1(3):195-197.

Walfish, S., Goplerud, E. N., and Broskowski, A. Survival strategies in community mental health: A study of management consensus. *American Journal of Orthopsychiatry*. 1986. 56(4):630-633.

Wamsley, G. L., and Zald, M. N. *The Political Economy of Public Organizations*. Lexington, MA: Lexington Books, 1973.

Wamsley, G. L., and Zald, M. N. The political economy of public organizations. *Public Administration Review*. 1973. 33:62-73.

Weatherley, R. Approaches to cutback management. In: F. D. Perlmutter, editor. *Human Services at Risk*. Washington, DC: Lexington Books, 1984.

Weinstein, H. P., and Leibman, M. S. Corporate scale down, what comes next? *Human Resource Magazine.* 1991. 36:33-37.

Wilburn, R. C., and Worman, M. A. Overcoming the limits to personnel cut-backs: Lessons learned in Pennsylvania. *Public Administration Review.* 1980. 41(1):21-28.